D1600203

MONA PARSONS

MONA PARSONS

From privilege to prison, from Nova Scotia to Nazi Europe

ANDRIA HILL

NIMBUS
PUBLISHING LTD

Nimbus Publishing Limited
PO Box 9301, Station A
Halifax, NS   B3K 5N5
(902) 455-4286

Design: Arthur Carter
Printed and bound in Canada

Canadian Cataloguing in Publication Data

Hill, Andria

  Mona Parsons

  ISBN 1-55109-293-X

1. Parsons, Mona, 1901-1976.   2. World War, 1939-1945 —
Underground movements — Netherlands — Biography.   3.
World War, 1939-1945 — Prisoners and prisons, German.   4.
Prisoners of war — Germany — Biography.   5. Prisoners of war
— Canada — Biography.   I. Title.

D802.N4H54 2000   940.53'492'092   C00-950195-9

Canadä

Nimbus Publishing acknowledges financial support for our publishing activities from the Government of Canada through the Book Publishing Industry Development Program (BPIDP), and the Canada Council.

Dedication
For my Caliban, Robbins Elliott

Main street in 1920s Wolfville: Mona Parsons' long journey would begin and end in this Nova Scotian town.

Contents

Acknowledgements

I would like to extend love, gratitude, and heartfelt thanks to all those who have enthusiastically supported and believed in the creation of this book. In particular, I want to acknowledge David McMullin for listening to what must have seemed interminable alternation between excitement and frustration; my children Maeghan, Garrow, Alex, James, Connor, and Una, for putting up with the highs and lows of the last few years, and for inquiring about my progress; my mother, Maye Preston-Hill, who supported me spiritually, creatively, and financially; Robbins Elliott, whose belief and interest helped find and facilitate the Dutch connections essential to complete this project; the phenomenal women of Seekhers Imports (Deb Harvey, Joann Garby, Angela Gélinas, Ayjai Young, Sara Munro, Rebecca Smith, and Michelle Waterbury) for their love, encouragement, and support; Shirley Elliott; Victoria Tufts Pickett; Adrian Potter; Wendelien van Holthe tot Echten van Boetzelaer; Marij van Donkelaar; Hans de Vries (RIOD); Robert Chesal (Radio Nederland); Gustav Leonhardt; Lie van Oldenborgh; "Joost"; the Rotary Clubs of Wolfville (Nova Scotia), Amersfoort, Apeldoorn, Delft, Laren, Vlissingen, Middelburg, Walcheren, and Groningen (Holland); Royal Canadian Legion, Dr. C.B. Lumsden Branch 74, Wolfville; Uwe Wilhelm; David Foster; Gillian Wickwire Pullen; Dr. Ron Stewart; Jane Evans; Pat Moore; Claudia Tugwell; Clyde MacDonald; Cathy MacRitchie; Wim and Tonnie van Beek; Dr.

Willem van Mourik; Baron and Baroness van Heeckeren; and to
Sarah Blenkhorn, André French, Andrew Gillis, and Samantha
Bissix, for "The Bitterest Time." I thank Dorothy Blythe, both for
giving me this opportunity and for remaining good humoured
and unflappable whenever I might have seemed "out there."
Thanks, too, to Clare Goulet, who helped midwife the last stage
of birthing this book. And last, but never least in my heart, I
thank Stephanie Domet, self-described "word nerd," but in my
eyes nothing less than the Goddess of the Blue Pencil.

Wolfville's Acadia University: the old stomping grounds of both Mona Parsons and
author Andria Hill, who first stumbled upon Mona's story while doing research
here in 1994.

Introduction

Reports of the final days of World War Two in Europe painted vivid pictures of triumph and despair, compassion and cruelty. Canadian soldiers fighting to liberate Holland raced to deliver food parcels to a nation brought to the brink of starvation during the Nazi occupation. In the small town of Vlagtwedde, near the German border in northeastern Holland, members of the North Nova Scotia Highlanders were astounded when an emaciated and sick woman approached them for help, and told them that, after nearly four years in Nazi prisons, she had walked across Germany following a desperate escape. Badly infected blisters on her bare feet were evidence of her two-week trek, but the soldiers were incredulous when she told them she was a Canadian—Mona Parsons, from Wolfville, Nova Scotia.

Although the story of Mona's ordeal was the source of several articles in Toronto's *Evening Telegram* in the months immediately following this discovery, her story was overshadowed by events unfolding in the rest of Europe and around the world. In the collective desire of the western world to recover a sense of normalcy after World War Two, Mona's story faded into the background; by the last decade of the twentieth century, it was recalled by only a few people, most of them residing in the town where she grew up. Mona's death in 1976 renewed local interest in her story, and in owning even a small part of her estate, which had been consigned to local antiques dealers. But once most of

these items had been sold, her story was once more relegated to
the shadows once more.

In 1994, I came across her story while searching for a topic for
my M.A. thesis in English. A brief article, written nearly 50 years
earlier for *The Acadia Bulletin*, gave a synopsis of her wartime
experiences. Convinced that a wealth of information must exist
in Wolfville—after all, one of its own had joined the early Dutch
resistance and been arrested by the Gestapo—I went looking for
more. Surprisingly, neither Acadia University's archives, nor
Wolfville's Historical Society could shed further light on Mona,
although several society board members assured me that they
knew of her. In fact, Robbins Elliott told me that not only did he
recall Mona when he was a young lad (his father had been the
Parsons family physician, and the Elliotts had lived around the
corner from them), but he remembered seeing her shortly after
her rescue in April 1945, while he was serving overseas. This
brought me tantalizingly close to a woman who would, over the
next six years, prove remarkably elusive.

By turns intrigued with Mona's story and frustrated that nothing more could be found, I went on with my thesis research,
promising myself that once it had been written and successfully
defended, I would pursue Mona's story—for the rest of my life, if
necessary. And, from early indications, there was a good possibility that such a length of time would be needed to piece things
together. Mona, however, seemed to have other ideas. And
because how the story unfolded was, at times, almost as remarkable as the story itself, this book will tell both.

The first lesson Mona taught me was that the way to immerse
myself in history was through a person. I'd studied theatre and
acting at Acadia, so Mona intrigued me not only as an individual, but also as a player on the world stage. Mona Parsons may
not have been widely influential like female war heroes Edith
Cavell or Mata Hari, but she was nonetheless significant. People
remembered her for her acting and singing talents, her vivacity
and beauty, her wit and charm, her lithe and graceful bearing,
and for having been ever-so-slightly scandalous. Because she had
died in 1976—eleven years before I moved to Nova Scotia—and
because there was almost no biographical information available,

I had to get to know her as I would a character in a play: by contemplating her life, trying on her persona, visualizing and imagining her, even venturing to fill in the blanks when no information seemed available. And, as in theatre, these exercises made me receptive to information on a subconscious level, which in turn yielded some surprising results.

One morning I arrived at the university archives to find someone occupying the space I usually used for research. I must have telegraphed my chagrin because the other researcher offered to move to another table. Feeling a little sheepish, I assured the woman that I could work at a different table. I shifted stacks on a nearby table and set up my papers and books. I was entering notes on a laptop computer when a stack of papers to my left began to slide onto my keyboard. I stopped them and then steadied the pile, but it was soon invading my workspace once again. After several unsuccessful attempts to stave off this invasion, I shoved the papers with more forcefully—then realized that this would send them cascading to the floor. I lunged to grab the papers before this happened, and stopped them just in time. But, in replacing the stack, my attention was caught by a piece of paper that had been near the bottom of the pile. It was the 1923 graduation programme for the Acadia Ladies Seminary. Mona had graduated in 1920. There were only a few more programmes. I uncovered the next—1922. The next—1921. Did I dare hope? The next—1920. I held it in my hands for a moment before flipping it open, my eyes instantly falling on a list of stories and poems that Mona Parsons recited at her graduation ceremonies. This was my first tangible sense of the young woman Mona had been, and the way in which this simple detail quietly but insistently revealed itself to me had a profound effect.

A year later, my thesis successfully defended, I turned to the detective work of reconstructing Mona's life. In the beginning, things looked promising. I approached the Wolfville Historical Society and offered to write a play about Mona as a fundraiser for the Society. I hoped that people with pieces of Mona's story would come forward to correct errors that were bound to appear in the script, because the information I had was so sketchy.

At that point, the most substantial information available was found in two books, published in 1953 and 1956, written by Richard Pape, one of the British airmen whom Mona and her husband Willem Leonhardt had helped escape occupied Holland. The story read like a script for a war-era propaganda film, where none of the characters were the least afraid of anything, and were always putting on a stiff upper lip in the face of incredible adversity. My mother—a Londoner who recalls the Blitz more clearly than she would care to—assures me that this was often the case; in retrospect, however, Pape's books seemed only to highlight what had been left out. Much of it didn't ring true, including the voice attributed to Mona. I believed that a great deal was missing, that Mona didn't sail through war, imprisonment, abuse, escape, and gut-wrenching episodes of near recapture without feeling something more than cramp in her incredibly stiff upper lip.

One humid, drizzly, June day, I was en route to a friend's apartment to work on the play about Mona. I drove along Ridge Road, with its view of the Minas Basin, and found myself thinking in very general terms about Mona. What had the area looked like when she was growing up in the early twentieth century? I imagined she must have walked or driven up to Ridge Stile Park, a popular picnic spot at the top of Highland Avenue. I wondered what her favourite season had been, or her favourite memories of Wolfville. Turning the car onto Gaspereau Avenue, which leads from Ridge Road into town, I passed Willowbank Cemetery, and my attention was attracted by a tall, white monument near the upper gate. An unaccountable feeling told me that the stone marked Mona's grave. Excited, I drove into the cemetery and parked near the monument, now partially obscured by a bush. As I drew closer, I could see the name "Parsons" in large letters carved on the monument. I stopped in my tracks and looked down at the ground. The marker in the wet earth indicated that I was standing on her grave. A chill went through me and I quickly stepped to one side, almost murmuring, "Excuse me." The stone marked a family plot, and the face I was looking at was a memorial to Mona's parents, Norval and Mary Parsons. The next face listed the names of Mona's brother Ross, and his wife, Mary. On the third face, I read that Mona's other brother, Gwynne, had died in Philadelphia in 1968 and that his body had been donated to medical science. Mona, on the other hand, had been remembered for all time as the wife of her second husband, who had been a major military figure in World War Two. They were married only five years before cancer claimed Harry Foster's life, and, although he is not interred with her, two of his many decorations appear on her epitaph. The stone is mute about Mona's wartime experiences and the citations for bravery she received after the war.

While the play about Mona Parsons was warmly welcomed by sold-out audiences for three performances in Wolfville, it was the Halifax audiences who affected me most profoundly. Seven people showed up on opening night, including a World War Two veteran who had volunteered to sell tickets for us, two young people of about 20, a few seniors, and a reporter from the *Chronicle-Herald*. Because our venue was small, we were able to see the faces of our audience (all of whom, with the exception of the reporter, were seated in the front row) as they rose to their feet for a standing ovation, tears streaming down their cheeks. Mona filled the room that night, and, for each person, her story had a different effect. Our small audience was willing to wait until we'd changed into street clothes to share this. For the two young Newfoundlanders, it was surprise which bordered on shame that they'd never learned about Mona Parsons and what she had endured. For the veteran, it was a similar feeling. He had served overseas and participated in the liberation of Holland, but never knew the role played by a Canadian woman in that country's early struggle against Nazism. And for one of the seniors, it was bittersweet memories of her own life in Holland during World War Two, combined with the heartfelt gratitude she had felt for all Canadians who came from a country so far away, to liberate hers.

A few times over the next few months I was approached by strangers who had seen the play and been captivated by Mona's story. One woman, Claudia Tugwell, told me she owned Mona's precious piano, urging me to visit her and see it. Although I knew the instrument had been very important to Mona, I hadn't thought much about it, and just had the idea firmly in my head that Mona's piano didn't have the standard black lacquer finish which most of us associate with grand pianos. Instead, I'd always imagined it as a honey colour.

It would be another year or so before I'd see it. Claudia had been recommended as a tutor for my daughter, and on our initial visit to the house, she ushered me to the conservatory where, in the lush greens of the decor and various plants, I first laid eyes on Mona's old piano. Standing at the keyboard, wishing I could play, a thought suddenly struck me. The piano was, indeed, a honey colour—oak—and not black lacquer. This was just sinking in when my eyes were drawn to some dark rings on the top, obviously created by wet glasses. These struck me as wrong. Following my gaze, Claudia hastily assured me that the rings had not been made by any carelessness on the part of her family. She said that when she had purchased the piano, she, too, had been surprised by the dark stains on such a beautifully crafted piece. Then she learned the history that had to be passed to each owner, as insurance that the stains would never be removed. While Mona languished in a Nazi prison camp, her home was occupied by officers of the Third Reich who made free use of the piano—including using the top of it as a table, leaving wet glasses on it while they enjoyed the music. On Mona's return home at the end of the war, she was indignant to discover the marks. But rather than have the piano stripped and the stains removed, she chose to leave them there as permanent testament to the wounds left on her soul by her harrowing wartime experience.

Author Andria Hill (*right*) interviews Mona's friend Lie van Oldenborgh in Holland. Van Oldenborgh visited Mona in Amstelveese prison, when the Canadian was first incarcerated for her resistance activities.

Chapter One

"a magical place"

When Norval Parsons married Mary Keith, she promised to love, honour, and obey him, and in return, he vowed to take care of her. The two met while growing up in Middleton, Nova Scotia in the 1870s. While he was still a child, Norval's parents had made the short move from his birthplace, Kingston, to Middleton. Mary's family had come from farther away—Salisbury, New Brunswick. And although Norval was sent to Horton Academy (a private school for young men in Wolfville, about 60 kilometres east of Middleton), he spent his holidays at home. Both the Parsons and Keith families attended the Baptist church and were active in the community, giving Norval and Mary lots of opportunity to become acquainted and, eventually, to fall in love.

Norval was in an excellent position to make good on his pledge to look after Mary: he was educated, ambitious, and had the necessary contacts to find employment without having to leave Nova Scotia. Mary's upbringing had prepared her to become an attentive and diligent wife, skilled at domestic duties. Following their marriage, each set out to do what was expected: as the manager of Parsons, Elliott Company, (a wholesale and retail hardware outlet), Norval provided the household income, while Mary organized their home and kept it running smoothly. Mary was active in church and community groups, while Norval dedicated himself to business interests and became a member of the Holy Royal Arch No. 16—a Masonic order.

Their first child, Matilda, was born in 1892, but did not survive infancy. Two years later, the Parsons had a son, Gwynne, and in 1896 their second son, Ross, arrived. Norval was delighted to have two sons to follow in his footsteps, sons who would look after their mother and her affairs if he died. Although Mary was happy to have two healthy sons, she couldn't help but wonder what her life might have been like had Matilda survived. A daughter might not be as useful as a son, but she could be a comfort to her mother. Mary dreamed of having a little girl whom she could teach to sew, to cook, and to manage a household; a little girl who would grow to womanhood, would in time become a wife and mother, and in turn would be comfort and companion to Mary in her old age. On February 17, 1901, Mary's prayers were answered with the birth of Mona Louise. As the baby of the family, Mona likely would have been indulged, and as the only girl this became a certainty. Perhaps because his first daughter had died in infancy, Norval was particularly attentive to Mona, and over the years they formed a close bond—though one not without conflict.

In 1911, the Parsons family was given an opportunity which, at first, seemed like a terrible setback. Norval's hardware business burned to the ground. Rather than rebuild, he accepted a position with the Brandram Henderson Company in Wolfville and moved his family into a comfortable, mansard-roofed house on Acadia Street. Wolfville was, and is, a university town; it has been since Acadia University's progenitor, Queen's College, was founded in 1838. But the history of Wolfville—or Mud Creek as it was known from about 1767 until 1830—can trace its origins back long before there ever was a Wolfville or a Mud Creek, back to the New England Planters, and before them, the Acadians. And even before the Acadians, there were the Mi'kmaq, whose history and rich culture have survived in the legends of gods and mortals from the time of Glooscap. This history and heritage were the essence of drama and romance, and appealed to young Mona's theatrical imagination.

At the time the Parsons family took up residence in Wolfville, the town had a population of two thousand; despite its modest size, two features gave Wolfville worldwide distinction. First, the tides of the Minas Basin at the top of the Bay of Fundy (on which Wolfville is located) were the highest in the world, lowering and raising water levels up to 60 feet every 13 hours. Second, Wolfville was home to the world's smallest registered harbour. Even more important to residents and visitors alike, Wolfville boasted some of the most beautiful natural scenery to be found anywhere. In 1912, mayor J.D. Chambers, writing about Wolfville's business potential, said that while "manufacturing had little success...the town (is) educational and residential, with good potential for the tourist industry." Except for the physical appearance of the town, nothing in that summary has changed since it was written nearly 90 years ago.

Photographs from the period show vestiges of locations which, ghost-like, are evoked in the town today: Main Street on a Saturday morning, the Duck Pond, buildings by the Wolfville harbour. The loss of many of the town's elm trees (abundantly evident in most photographs of Main Street from this time) has transformed the town dramatically since Mona's childhood. Landmarks in some photographs no longer exist, such as the stately, neo-classical, stone building which once housed the post office. Looking at these old photographs, it is easy to imagine young Mona Parsons walking along Main Street, running an errand for her mother, perhaps at Rand's Drug Store, or through the T. Eaton mail-order outlet in town. While the Wolfville of the first three decades of the twentieth century might be difficult to find in town today, the Wolfville where Mona Parsons spent the final years of her life in the 1970s is easier to imagine. If Mona were to return to Wolfville today, her experience might be like that of meeting an old friend—changed, but reassuringly familiar in some aspects.

The Parsons family joined the Wolfville Baptist Church, which boasted such a large congregation that a new church had to be built the year after the family took up residence in town. Mary became involved in the activities of most women of her station, giving card parties and afternoon teas for other women in the community, and in turn attending those hosted by others. Wolfville's weekly newspaper, *The Acadian*, faithfully recorded these social exchanges and other items of community importance, including the travels of leading members and their children, and the names of those receiving visits from family and friends not resident in Wolfville. While a young, single man, Norval had enjoyed the dashing image that came with his membership in the King's Canadian Hussars (a reserve militia unit). However, as a husband and father, he became a more sedate, responsible provider as a businessman. He eventually became a representative of the Nova Scotia Trust Company, and lent a hand in the organization of the Maritime Finance Company. By the time World War One was declared, he listed his occupation as stock broker.

Wolfville was a prosperous community. Its streets were the first in the province to be paved with tar, and the town even boasted a few paved sidewalks. Grocers, stables, dry goods merchants, milliners, dressmakers and tailors, an ice cream parlour, jewellers, druggists, dentists and doctors provided some of the necessities and a few of the niceties of life. Several people and a few businesses owned automobiles, driven on the left-hand side of the road in the British fashion—a practice which changed in 1920 with the increased number of Americans driving their automobiles on Canadian roads. Wolfville was a stop on the railway line that carried passengers on the three-and-a-half hour trip to Halifax, to neighbouring communities, or to other provinces and the United States.

If it was entertainment that residents wanted, there was no need to look much farther than the town limits, especially in the spring and summer months. College Hall provided some of the theatrical entertainment, and performers were in abundant supply: students from Acadia, Horton Acadamy (Norval was an alummus of both) and the Ladies Seminary, Wolfville residents and even the occasional touring company. Popular tunes, favourite waltzes, and familiar marches filled the air in spring and summer when the community band performed on a bandstand on Main Street. The same group, and occasionally ensembles from neighbouring towns, played at dances held with some regularity at the Wolfville Community Hall. Tied up at the town wharf was a ferry that took passengers on excursions as far away as Parrsboro. In fine weather, people could go to Kingsport or

Evangeline Beach for the day, or pack a picnic lunch and head up Highland Avenue to The Stile, where views of the Minas Basin stretched out on one side of the ridge, with the Gaspereau Valley on the other.

Brand new to Main Street the year Mona and her family became residents of Wolfville was a particularly magical place called The Opera House. With a capacity of between 500 and 700 seats, The Opera House had modern conveniences: steam heat, electric lights, two film projectors, and a telephone connecting box office and stage. There was moveable scenery and backstage dressing rooms, so the space could be used either for live theatre or for moving pictures. The first opera, At the Cross Roads, was staged in July 1911. Imagine an enthralled ten-year-old Mona Parsons in the audience at that gala première performance, which attracted the leading citizens of Wolfville, resplendent in their summer finery, fanning themselves in the theatre's still interior.

The Opera House was a favourite stop for touring companies like The Colonial Stock Company, whose plays were popular because they were "clean and wholesome with a good moral tone" and Perry's Peerless Players, who offered plays with vaudeville entertainment between acts. Acadia University's Fine Arts Programme (which, in its present incarnation, is called the Acadia Performing Arts Series) used the space for musical performers and visiting lecturers, such as a screening of Dante's Inferno in February 1912, boasting "Lecturer, Effects, Special Music" for the price of 25, 35, or 50 cents per ticket. In April of that year, Wolfville was treated to the inimitable Sarah Bernhardt's screen performance in Dumas's Camille. Vitagraph Monthly provided reels of current events for public showings, and later the events of World War One were brought to the community on Pathé newsreels. Between the newspapers and the newsreels, Mona and her neighbours kept current with developments beyond Wolfville and Nova Scotia.

Life didn't stop for winter, though it might have slowed down a little. In the early seventeenth century, after spending a winter in the Atlantic region, Samuel de Champlain ruefully observed that the season could be six months long. Even if that's an exaggeration, there is little doubt that winters occasionally seemed interminable. But as Champlain's contemporaries found, long days and even longer nights of cold, miserable weather, could be made tolerable—even enjoyable—with the right entertainment. Skating was one of the most popular forms of entertainment when Mona Parsons was a young resident of Wolfville. There was no shortage of rinks, from the surface of the frozen duck pond at one end of town, to an area cleared on the school grounds. The most popular and largest surface in town was the Evangeline Rink, site of fancy dress carnivals and masquerades that were highlights of the winter, anticipated with great excitement each year. And Mona loved to skate—a passion which she carried into her adult life, when she was able to skate on canals in Holland and outdoor rinks in Switzerland. But some of the excitement she must have felt as a youth about the annual ice events in Wolfville can be surmised from descriptions carried in the pages of The Acadian. As many as a thousand people were drawn to these events—that's half the population of the town at the time—with up to five hundred arriving on special trains from Kentville, Berwick, Middleton, Windsor, and other communities beyond Wolfville. The rink was specially decorated for these occasions, and bands from Wolfville or other local communities such as Kentville and Berwick provided music, though at least once the Royal Canadian Military Band performed.

But life in Wolfville wasn't just theatre, concerts, and carnivals. Service groups, clubs, and organizations formed an important part of the community's core. Thirteen-year-old Mona joined the first Camp Fire Girls group established in Wolfville in April 1914, just months before the outbreak of World War One. The group of 21 young women met in the ample and well-appointed residence of their leader, Waittie Stackhouse, using a room on the first floor of the three-storey home at 369 Main Street. For its name, the group adopted "Gluscap," the ancient god of aboriginal legends. Mona was tested with other girls in the areas of "Health, Crafts, Business, and Patriotism"—requirements for membership in the group. As part of their contribution to relief activities during World War One, members made clothes for Belgian babies.

Valley girl: Born in Middleton, N.S. in 1901, Mona moved to Wolfville with her family in 1911, where this picture of her as a young girl was taken. Below are her parents—her mother, Mary Keith of Salisbury, New Brunswick, met Colonel Norval Parsons in Middleton in the 1870s.

Growing up in Wolfville, in Nova Scotia's Annapolis Valley. *Clockwise from top*: Mona as a girl with parents Norval and Mary Parsons; walking with her father on the dykes; posing in her snowshoes.

Mona was enrolled in the junior school of the Acadia Ladies Seminary, whose catalogue proclaimed a commitment "to developing a simple, cultured, genteel Christian type of womanhood in accordance with the best ideals of the Churches." Mona, however, quickly developed a reputation for being wilful, independent, and outspoken—qualities she inherited or copied from her father. But she also had a vivid imagination and creative talent which she put to use through acting, music, dancing, painting, and gardening. Although Mona's temperament and horticultural abilities were the result of her father's influence and tutelage, little apart from her love of cooking could be attributed to her mother. A photograph of Mary Keith Parsons shows a handsome woman with her hair sedately wound around her head in the fashion of a slightly earlier day, clad in a dark dress with a long string of beads trailing down the front, her hands clasped demurely in front of her. Mary fulfilled the traditional wife-and-mother role. If she ever had any aspirations or inclinations outside the domestic duties for which every woman of her generation had been raised, Mona never knew about it. One woman, Victoria Tufts, a close neighbour, and daughter of renowned naturalist Robie Tufts, recalls that Mary Parsons was pleasant but could well have been part of the wallpaper. Mary deferred to her husband in all matters, a tendency that did not escape the notice of young Mona, and that informed the adult she would become.

As Mona grew older and watched her brothers undertake exciting careers (Ross in Australia with the Nicholson File Company, and Gwynne in Philadelphia with the National Press), her rich imagination helped her see that there were more possibilities than wife and mother. Helpful, too, was the fact that Mona entered adolescence during World War One. Never had the nation known such a war, where fighting for one's country started off as a romantic ideal, but often resulted in broken people, shattered dreams, and a generation deprived of the beautiful idealism and possibilities that belong to youth. The end of World War One heralded a period of carefree living that bordered on the reckless. A generation aged before its time was constantly ready to fly in the face of those who would condemn it the price it had paid on the battlefields of Europe.

While the military actively recruited men through an office in Wolfville, the community got involved in the war effort. Townspeople threw themselves into a variety of war-related activities, from women who bottled extra preserves to send overseas, to the local Boy Scout troop, whose facilities were used for temporary military housing. Town council voted to invest $2,500 in Victory Bonds, and various girls' and women's clubs organized special events and drives to raise funds for the war effort. Mona dutifully and patriotically did her part, knitting outfits for Belgian babies and socks for British soldiers. But she also read diverging essays written by students at the Acadia Ladies Seminary, some condemning women who supported the suffrage movement, and other rhapsodizing about the women who "donned khaki and spurs" and headed for the battlefields of France. Closer to home, women took over businesses and ran farms while fathers, husbands, and brothers fought a war in a distant land, which gave Mona reason to wonder why she should accept the domestic roles most women, up to that point, had been expected to fulfill without question. True, there were women who had careers, such as teachers or secretaries, but few chose this because they desired an independent lifestyle. Some were waiting to find a husband (still the best chance for security in those days), and others, like Blanche Lehigh McLean, who would be one of Mona's drama teachers, went to work after their husbands died.

Like every other community across Canada, Wolfville was transformed by World War One. In the beginning, the war in Europe was seen as a just and glorious cause. A recruiting office opened on Main Street; posters covering the glass front bore messages such as "You said you would go when you were NEEDED, and you are needed NOW!" and "Send more men—Will YOU answer the call?" Outside, a sandwich board entreated male passers-by to "Halt!" and consider enlisting in the local regiment of the Nova Scotia Highlanders—the West Nova Scotia Regiment out of nearby Aldershot. Norval Parsons was three months shy of his forty-seventh birthday in 1916 when he deducted two years from his age, filled out enlistment forms and was permitted to join the Canadian Overseas Expeditionary Force. Appointed temporary Major of the 85th Battalion mobilized out of Camp Aldershot, Nova Scotia in May 1916, he achieved the rank of Lieutenant Colonel upon transfer to the 246th Battalion. Until his death in the 1950s, Norval would ever after be known as The Colonel by Mona—a combination of affection and affectation. Ross and Gwynne were both old enough for military service, and they, too, enlisted in the army. Norval's tour of duty overseas was limited to England, where he arrived in June 1917, and he returned to Canada in October of the same year. Miraculously, considering the high casualty rate in that war, all three Parsons men returned home, although Ross was wounded at Lens in 1917 (months after graduating from Acadia University) and received the Military Medal for Bravery. Wolfville's delight at having an end to the war at last was tempered by the reality that many young men would not return home, even for burial. Sombre plans were made for appropriate war memorials in town and on campus.

In the meantime, Mona's natural inclination for attention, and her abundant self-confidence, led her to the performing arts. At the age of 15, she was tall and willowy, without a hint of the gangliness that often overshadows these attributes at an early age, and she was thoroughly captivating. Her speaking voice was measured and understated, and her singing voice almost smoky, beginning to take on the husky tones that would be its mark of distinction in adulthood. After completing her education at the junior school of the Seminary, she enrolled in its Conservatory of Music and Fine Arts. There, she pursued a diploma in Oratory and Expression. Requirements included "Collegiate Courses" in standard academic subjects like math, Latin, and sciences, as well as psychology, logic, and ethics. The course for a diploma in expression spanned three years, during which time students took private and group classes in expression, as well as lessons in movement, the Delsarte method, pantomime, "platform deportment," and voice. Each year, students increased their knowledge of the organs and processes associated with voice and enunciation. Required reading included Shakespeare, epic and lyric poetry (including the works of Thomas Ruskin, Thomas Carlyle, Elizabeth Barrett, and Robert Browning), Bible and hymnal

Mona's early dramatic education would serve her well in her escape across Nazi Germany. *Above*: Seminary House, formerly the Acadia Ladies Seminary, where Mona studied music, dance, theatre, and literature, graduating in May 1920. *Centre*: University Hall, home to the stage on which Mona appeared in several productions including the 1928 musical *Buddies*.

The Honor Dramatic Fraternity
of
Acadia University

presents

THE MERRY MUSIC PLAY

"BUDDIES"

The play by George V. Hobart
The Lyrics and Music by B. C. Hilliam

DON WETMORE—Director

UNIVERSITY HALL
TUESDAY EVENING, APRIL 24, 1928

passages, and works of dramatic literature. Students were given opportunities in class to speak extemporaneously on assigned topics, and to display their skills in public recitals. In addition to her studies in expression, Mona learned to sing and to play the piano. She learned classical pieces, but her musical tastes inclined toward the popular tunes of the day. Mona loved to read, and she had a prodigious memory that enabled her to learn long passages—many which she was able to recall easily throughout her life. It was a skill that would comfort her, in time, allowing her to distance herself from the grim reality of Nazi prisons.

While Mona hadn't ruled out the idea of eventual marriage, she certainly didn't intend to undertake this until she'd lived a little. Her enrollment in the Conservatory of Music and Fine Arts wasn't reason for her family to panic. No, with a background in music and fine arts, a woman could secure a respectable position as a teacher, and after marriage, provide a nice touch in the drawing room. But at the Conservatory of Fine Arts, two women would play a role in the direction of Mona's career aspirations. One was Cora Pierce Richmond, one of Mona's voice teachers. Strong and independent, Richmond, a widow, had been appointed to the Acadia Ladies' Seminary faculty around 1912. Her reputation as an excellent music teacher grew, and she decided to open a studio in downtown Wolfville that would allow students outside the seminary to benefit from her teaching. Administrators at the seminary balked, citing a potential conflict and competition with the school's programme (though the seminary accepted students from the community, not regularly enrolled in other classes, to take some of its courses in domestic science). Richmond stood her ground and the private studio on Main Street flourished. Cora Pierce Richmond had been trained in Boston, and a number of her students went on to pursue professional voice careers. Of those who remained in the local area, many were in demand for public recitals and church functions. With Richmond's influence, Wolfville's Opera House became the venue for several musicals and operettas over the years, including a production of Gilbert and Sullivan's *HMS Pinafore*, in which Mona had a role. Mona went on to perform in several

plays and musicals in Wolfville, treating the audience to her
lovely alto voice.

The second strong role model for Mona's career aspirations
was Blanche Lehigh McLean. The widow of a prominent Cape
Breton physician, McLean taught expression and voice in
Halifax for a few years before joining the faculty of Acadia
University. Accompanied by her four children, she took up residence in Wolfville and became one of the people who most
influenced the course of Acadia's and Nova Scotia's theatre history. During her tenure as an instructor, and later as Dean of
Women, McLean was a strong advocate of theatre arts, and was
instrumental in establishing at Acadia University a chapter of an
international dramatic fraternity open to both men and women.
Though Mona Parsons was never listed as one of the fraternity's
members, she acted in some of its productions, and certainly
attended its other performances. McLean was also a proponent of
the philosophy of the Little Theatre Movement, which had started in Europe around the turn of the century, reached New York
in 1912, and found a strong voice in American theatre companies like The Provincetown Players, the Washington Square
Players, and The Theatre Guild. Largely inspired by McLean's
efforts, many of the plays produced by these companies were
eventually produced on the Acadia campus—most notably the
works of Eugene O'Neill—long before they appeared elsewhere
in Nova Scotia.

McLean's daughter, Kathlyn ("Tat") was a few years younger
than Mona, but they appeared together in a few local theatre and
music productions, along with some of the other McLean children. After graduating from the Ladies Seminary, both Kathlyn
and Mona pursued further studies in voice and expression in
1925, though at different schools—Kathlyn in Toronto, and Mona
in the United States. Kathlyn followed her mother's example and
became a teacher of expression and voice. She taught drama in
West Virginia and in Saint John, New Brunswick, and briefly
became reacquainted with Mona when both women returned to
Wolfville in the late 1920s, where they were active in the local
theatre scene. But Kathlyn's dreams of a stage career changed
when she married Ira Beatty and settled down to raise two chil-

dren. Her love of theatre, though, remained, and she inspired her children—known to movie-lovers as Shirley MacLaine and Warren Beatty—to pursue professional theatre careers.

By her final year of studies at the Ladies' Seminary, Mona was beautiful, lithe, and moved with an easy grace that was almost hypnotic. A portrait of her captured a classically-beautiful woman with an oval face and porcelain skin, framed by dark, wavy hair pulled back from her face and loosely gathered at the base of her neck. Her large, dark, expressive eyes gaze off camera at something that prompts her perfectly-drawn, Clara Bow mouth to purse in the vaguest hint of a smile (or perhaps exasperation). As a resident student at the seminary for the 1919-1920 academic year—her final year—she was required to to join the Pierian Society, a club dedicated to the furtherance of young women's appreciation of Literature, and to the honing of literary talent. The society published a magazine, *The Pierian*, three or four times a year, which featured the poetry, prose, essays, and jokes of its membership. Mona's contribution for the year appeared in the November 1919 issue, a brief scene entitled "My Busy Day"—a parody of the stereotypical housewife, overwrought by domestic duties, unable to cope with getting her child off to school for the day, and helpless without a scullery maid. In March, one of Mona's classmates, Flora Manning, contributed a brief item as an "in-joke," and one that leaves no doubt that, not only was Mona turning male heads, she was thoroughly enjoying her carefully-calculated effect: "Miss Parsons seems very fond of the Dexter Millinery Parlours during the past week. There are rumours about that the assistant is not a female."

Mona was also a romantic whose imagination was captured by poetry, painting, and beautiful prose. Prior to receiving her diploma in Expression, she was required to perform selected pieces at a public recital held in College Hall at 8 P.M. on May 18, 1920. Her four pieces were: "Cherry Blossoms," by Van Tassel Sutphen; "Limpy: a story", by William Johnson; "How It Happened," a monologue by Marjorie Benton Cooke; and the poem "Patterns," by Amy Lowell. Though little is known about the authors of the first pieces, Amy Lowell was renowned as an Imagist poet; she was also a feminist who came under a great deal of criticism from the establishment of the day. Lowell, who died in 1925 at the age of 54, favoured garden imagery in her poems, which were frequently erotic and, in her later works, unabashedly lesbian. "Patterns," however, is a condemnation of the waste of young lives during war. Doubtless it was one of the poems which came unbidden to Mona's mind during her incarceration during World War Two:

And the softness of my body will be guarded from embrace
By each button, hook, and lace.
For the man who should loose me is dead,
Fighting with the Duke in Flanders,
In a pattern called a war.
Christ! What are patterns for?

Although Mona carefully studied and understood the effect of every gesture and nuance she made, she was also genuine and unaffected. Her grace and friendliness fascinated younger women almost as much as her beauty and stylishness.

"Mona had on a lovely black dress—sort of a silky crêpe material, one that didn't rustle crisply but rather swished a bit when she walked," recalls Shirley Elliott. A neighbour who lived nearby on Linden Avenue, Shirley's father was the Parsons's family physician. "We were spellbound as she walked up Linden Avenue toward Acadia Street! She moved with such grace and ease. We called out to her, and she smiled and waved with the same ease and grace she walked with. She didn't wave her hand vigorously, but hailed us with a slow, smooth, graceful movement of her hand and forearm."

The small group of friends were so captivated by the way Mona carried herself that they decided to ask her for dance lessons. Shirley, several years Mona's junior, shyly approached the young woman with the group's request, and was delighted when Mona agreed.

"I arrived at the Parsons house on Acadia Street," Shirley recalls. "Knocking on the door, I was admitted by Mona's mother and she told me that Mona would be downstairs shortly. As I stood in their front hall, I could see Mona's black pumps lying where she had kicked them off the night before. Her wrap was hanging over the bottom of the banister. I remembered that she had said she was going to a dance at, I think, Camp Aldershot the night before. In a short while, Mona came down the stairs and we went into the large double front parlour at the left off the front hall. I helped her roll back the carpets and move the furniture to prepare for our dance lesson. Then she put a record on the gramophone, and the lesson began. I can't recall all the tunes she taught me to dance to, but one I do recall as one of her favourites was "I Can't Give You Anything But Love," which was a very popular dance tune of the time."

Mona firmly believed that not only should a woman be able to move with confidence, grace, and ease, but that she should also learn to express herself well. Possessed of a delightful speaking voice that bordered on sultry, she offered lessons in elocution and expression, as well as dancing. She not only taught neighbourhood girls and young women to speak clearly, she helped them to speak with calm and poise on various topics. Victoria Tufts was one of the younger women in Wolfville for whom Mona represented the highest aspirations of womanliness. "I don't think she really knew what she was doing, or that she had taken special training to be an instructor," Victoria says now. "She simply had a natural talent, and she was happy to share it with others."

In addition to being a dancer and having a lovely speaking and singing voice, Mona had other talents. She loved to cook. And Victoria Tufts was a willing pupil. Even more than having Mona teach her the hesitation waltz ("one, two, three, pause, then twirl around"), Victoria savours the memory of Mona teaching her to bake a chocolate cake that produced mouth-watering results; Victoria continued to use the recipe as an adult. Heavenly smells of chocolate filled the Parsons kitchen on Acadia Street as Mona showed the younger woman how to measure the flour, the sugar, the butter, then combine them with other ingredients to create a rich, chocolate batter. The aroma of the nearly-finished product, baking in the oven, was such that Victoria could still relish its effect more than 70 years later. Little wonder, then, that Mona's cooking talents were among those that

played a significant role in the strategies she developed to survive Nazi prisons during World War Two.

In the September following her graduation from the Acadia
Ladies Seminary, Mona—possibly influenced by voice teacher
Cora Pierce Richmond—enrolled at the Currie School of
Expression in Boston. Not only did this enable her to further her
training, but it also allowed her to live a significant distance
away from home for the first time. Although Mona was a diligent
student intent on doing well, she also loved a good party.
Prohibition, which had been introduced to the United States and
Canada in 1917 as part of the war effort, was still in effect in the
United States in 1920 (and would be until 1933), and that meant
the temptation of things not only forbidden, but illegal:
speakeasies, bathtub gin, and bootleggers. Mona might not have
had her first introduction to bootleggers in Boston, but she likely
went to her first speakeasy while living there.

These were heady times, in the wake of World War One, as
mass-marketing through the relatively-new medium of radio,
along with the first opportunities to buy on credit, allowed the
average person to indulge in more consumer goods than ever
before. Added to that was an almost desperate need for novelty,
and the free-living, free-loving Bohemianism of cultural icons
such as Pablo Picasso, F. Scott Fitzgerald, Isadora Duncan, and
Dorothy Parker. Society was a far cry from that of pre-war, where
art and culture were focused on life as it should be. Youth was
more aware than ever that life could be cut short, and it was
determined both to portray life as it was, and to live it to the
fullest. The 1920s brought The Jazz Age and the era of the
Flapper, with her bobbed hair, short skirts, revealing necklines,
rolled-down stockings (or none at all!), and dramatic make-up—
white face powder, red lips, and black eyeliner reminiscent of
the Egyptian craze that followed the discovery of King Tut's
tomb. Like many young women who enjoyed this new era of
freedom, Mona also indulged in cigarettes.

Although popular magazines, such as *The New Republican* or
Outlook, embraced these trends, encouraging the older generation to try to understand the needs of youth, Mona's parents
were alarmed by their daughter's whole-hearted embrace of pop-

ular culture. They still hoped that Mona would find a good husband, but she was not yet ready to settle down. Instead of returning to Wolfville once she had completed her studies at the Currie School of Expression, she sought more training, farther afield, at Central College, in Conway, Arkansas. Although her reasons for choosing this Baptist college so far from home are not clear, Mona studied voice and music at Central College for two years, leaving in 1925. She returned to Wolfville, where she met up again with Tat McLean, who had also returned home after studying in Toronto and teaching in New Brunswick. They became involved once again in local theatre activities, mostly on the Acadia campus. But not too much time elapsed before Tat left for another teaching job, this time in Virginia, and Mona felt the need for a place that offered more excitement. She turned her attention to New York, and contemplated a career in professional theatre.

Over the years, Mona offered different versions of her break into show biz in New York City. In one version, she claims to have seen Florenz Ziegfeld—impresario of the city's largest, and probably most expensive, musical and theatrical revue in the twentieth century-dining in a fashionable New York restaurant, and brazenly asked him for an audition. Given Mona's reputation for being forthright, and Ziegfeld's appreciation for a pretty face, a nicely turned leg, and a sultry voice, the scenario is entirely believable. In a more tame version, Mona claimed that she had auditioned for, and been cast in, a touring show of the Follies. No matter how she got there, she played the part to the hilt, dyeing her brunette locks blonde in the popular fashion of some of the leading starlets of stage and screen. But though she played the part, her heart wasn't in it. Inspired by Blanche Lehigh McLean's promotion of the Little Theatre Movement, Mona was more inclined toward a role in serious theatre. The New York theatres that espoused and represented that movement (which had been born from a disdain of Victorian melodrama and the star system of theatre) were going strong. But, despite her considerable talent for singing, dancing, and acting, Mona would not become a star of the stage.

Although she attracted the attention of several wealthy men, she grew bored with dangling from their arms. Before she could

A long way from Wolfville: New York City in the heyday of the 1920s—jazz, flappers, and the Ziegfeld Follies. Mona Parsons worked here as an actress, chorus girl, and Park Avenue nurse before her brother Ross (in nearby Rhode Island) introduced her to millionaire Willem Leonhardt, whom she promptly took on a tour of the city.

Chorus girl Mona in 1920s New York: Mona gave several versions of her entrance to the chorus line of the famed Ziegfeld Follies; in one of these, she claimed to have seen Florenz Ziegfeld (*bottom right*) in a New York restaurant, where she brazenly asked him for an audition. *Below*: Ziegfeld chorus dancers perform his 1920s production of *Sally*.

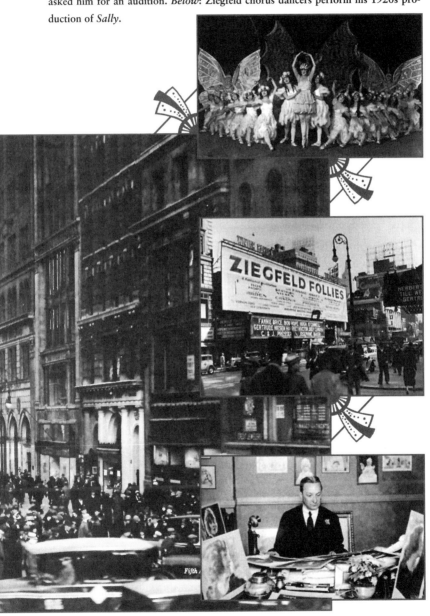

pursue other options, life presented her with an opportunity to tear up her contract—and doubtless, had Mona had another choice, she would gladly have taken the second option. In February of 1930, she received an urgent telegram summoning her home at once. Her mother had suffered a stroke. Although Mary did not approve of Mona's choice of a career in show business, and though neither woman understood the other well, Mona loved her mother. Perhaps she even felt a little sorry for her. Though Mona adored her father, she must have pitied her mother's virtual enslavement in a domestic role. Mary Parsons might not have viewed her life in that light, but Mona abhorred the thought of following in her mother's footsteps; she hoped to marry one day, but would not dream of becoming a domestic adjunct to her husband.

By the time Mona arrived back in Wolfville, Mary had rallied a little. She was conscious and in good spirits. At the suggestion of Dr. Elliott, a private nurse named Alma Cumming had been hired to care for Mary. Friends and neighbours offered prayers and wishes for a speedy recovery for Mary, but it was not to be. The day after Mona's twenty-ninth birthday, Mary Parsons suffered a second and fatal stroke. Alma, who was six years older than Mona, was a quiet and gentle woman who provided the support that Mona and her family needed. A friendship between the two women would become even stronger when, seven months after Mary Parsons died, Norval Parsons married Alma. But in the period immediately following Mary's death, Mona gave some serious thought to her future. By the popular standards of a society that exulted in youth, Mona was getting old. Her days as a show girl were rapidly coming to an end. Although she returned to New York, she knew she had to find something else. Her prospects for starting a career in serious theatre weren't very good. The stock market crash of a few months earlier had taken a toll, both on the glittering revues of Broadway (though budget cutbacks on such lavish productions were hardly noticeable), and on the art theatres with smaller budgets. And it wasn't just theatres that were suffering. Everywhere the effects of the Great Depression were beginning to be felt. No one could have imagined that the heady times of the Roaring Twenties were over for good, nor that it would take so long to pull out of the slump that was the Dirty Thirties.

Perhaps partly influenced by Alma Cumming Parsons, and partly by the memory of the praises sung of World War One nurses, Mona finally decided to put behind her a career in theatre, and become a nurse. In later years, Mona would claim there was nothing terribly humanitarian in her decision—she was ready to get married, and she wasn't going to find a suitable partner among the broke high-rollers she'd once dated. The best place to meet eligible men was in the health care profession, with a respectable, Florence Nightingale-esque career. Accordingly, she enrolled in the Jersey City Medical School, from which she graduated in 1935 with a high honours certificate, and was offered employment in the office of a Park Avenue ear, nose, and throat specialist—an expatriate Nova Scotian named Ross Faulkner. Although most of the country was still in the deepest part of the Depression, Mona established herself as an independent career woman in one of North America's most cosmopolitan cities. She was still interested in finding a husband, but there was no need to hurry. She was content to enjoy everything that New York had to offer while waiting for the right man to come along.

February was a memorable month for Mona: her birthday fell on the seventeenth of that month, she'd lost her mother in that month, and, in 1937, February would provide her with an experience that would change her life. Her brother Ross, who lived in the United States as a director of the Nicholson File Company, telephoned to ask Mona if she would act as hostess for a business acquaintance who was visiting from Holland. (The Nicholson File Company's head office was in Rhode Island, and would later facilitate movement of Mona's mail from Nazi-occupied Holland in 1940 to Ross and to her father in Canada). Always ready for a night of dining and dancing, especially when her companion was a suave and sophisticated European, Mona accepted. Not only was Willem Leonhardt all that, he was also an unmarried millionaire, visiting the United States and Mexico on behalf of his firm, Peck & Company—a business which provided top-of-the-line plumbing fixtures to the European market. Although the thought of a rich, plumbing fixtures salesman might make some

With no idea of the looming war they're heading into, Mona and Willem leave North America in August of 1937. *Top*: a newly-engaged Mona and Willem visit her father in Halifax. *Centre*: the couple at a party on board ship, the night before they sail for Holland. *Left*: an Art Deco-style advertisement for Bremen's luxury 1930s liners.

smile, Leonhardt's business was no joke. His family had started the company in the 1850s, when Amsterdam began to lay the groundwork for its modern plumbing systems. Once that job was complete—and the family fortune established—the company diversified to provide the equipment necessary to keep all the attendant pumps and lines in good order. Then, with the end of World War One, and the sudden "discovery" of the bathroom (prior to the war it had been unmentionable in polite company) as a place of potential relaxation and even leisure, the company experienced another jump in growth. Hollywood, especially, was intent on showing the world how opulent bathrooms could be, and the elite competed for the most incredible bathrooms. Firms like Peck & Company offered clients the latest in fixtures, colours, and designs.

Mona, in her vivacious style, happily showed Willem the best of New York—theatre, dinner, the Empire State Building, the Statue of Liberty. The two shared a love for jazz and so certainly went to a club or two in Harlem. Altough Willem had travelled considerably, he'd been raised in Dutch society which was, at the time, very formal, and had been educated in British boarding schools, which could be equally stuffy. Mona was three years older that Willem (a fact that surprised some who knew them, because the quieter, reserved, more circumspect Willem seemed many years her senior), and she captivated him with her spontaneity and zest for life, which must have been like fresh air and sunshine when compared with Dutch upper-class society. Although Willem continued his tour of the US and Mexico, he made sure that he returned to New York to enjoy more of Mona's company before returning to Holland. The brief tour gave sufficient time for the full effect of Mona's personality to work as a tonic on him, and, upon his return to New York, they became engaged. In April, they made a quick trip to Nova Scotia so Willem could meet Norval and Alma before he headed back to Amsterdam. A wedding date was set for September 1 (the period from Norval and Alma's first meeting to the time they married was the same—just over six months), and at the end of July, Willem returned to New York to accompany Mona to Holland for the nuptials. A photograph taken on board the ship the night before they sailed on the New York-Bremen line shows Mona and Willem happily chatting with other passengers, and conveys the luxury of ocean travel for those with the means to do it. Willem sent a postcard to Norval Parsons from the ship, saying they were enjoying the trip, and that he hoped Norval was feeling better. (Evidently, whatever ailed Norval was sufficient to prevent him from attending the wedding.) As soon as they arrived in Holland, Mona dispatched a telegram to her father to say that she had met the family and liked them immensely.

In much the same tradition that a woman about to marry into the British Royal Family resides in one of the palaces in the weeks prior to the wedding, Mona's first home was that of her future in-laws: Schoonord, in s'Graveland. The home is still a local landmark, with its three storeys and enormous, sloping, thatched roof. At the time Willem's parents owned it, the house was surrounded by expanses of lawn, fields, a lake, and greenhouses, and was home to various livestock that supplied the family with eggs, butter, and meat. Mona was assigned a maid, Gertrude, who attended to her personal needs—something that was doubtless appreciated as Mona was introduced to family, friends, and business associates at what must have seemed an endless round of luncheons, receptions, and dinners. Even Mona, who loved to socialize, must have been exhausted by the proceedings. Any observer, especially most of those whom Mona knew in North America, would have thought that Mona had found her Prince Charming, and that it only remained for her to live happily ever after.

Willem Leonhardt's green Jaguar parked outside Schoonord, his parent's estate in s'Graveland. *Inset*: Victoire and Georg Leonhardt, Willem's parents.

Chapter Two

"conjuring images"

T he details of Mona Parson's life were tangible yet elusive from the moment I found the first fragment of her story. I knew that important pieces were to be found in Holland, but I had no idea how I would begin to find them. Through the dogged determination of Robbins Elliott, son of the Parsons family's physician, I was finally able to travel to Holland in April 1998. The first day of the research and speaking tour promised to be something of a marathon. Robbins and I flew first to Reykjavik, then to Amsterdam. Our plane touched down at 11:00 A.M.—in plenty of time, I thought, to make it to Hilversum to record an interview for later broadcast on Radio Nederland. Even though we had taken into account that we'd likely get lost, we still arrived twenty minutes past our appointed time and dashed into the studios. Robert, our host at Radio Nederland, greeted us warmly, and told us not to worry about the time, except insofar as it affected our next appointment—my first speaking engagement was scheduled in Apeldoorn at 5:00 P.M. (Much to our surprise, Robbins and I arrived right on time.)

What little I had seen of Holland in those first few hours impressed me as a thoroughly modern country. Notably absent were the windmills I'd expected. Old farmhouses with tiled roofs dotted the countryside as we sped along ample highways. The impression was unchanged by the time we reached Apeldoorn, where we navigated tidy, tree-lined streets in search of the

Konigskroon Hotel. Lushly landscaped and elegant, the Konigskroon sits in a modern section of the city. Once inside, we were greeted by our host and president of the local Rotary Club, Michiel. There was no time to develop any pre-talk jitters as I was introduced to several members of the club. My relief at discovering they all spoke perfect English was tinged with some embarrassment that I had not even learned the most basic greeting in Dutch. That didn't seem to matter at all to anyone, as they warmly greeted Robbins, who had been one of their liberators. It didn't take long for me to think of that word with a capital "L," and I find it impossible to think of it otherwise, as I heard countless people tell him, "Thank you, Liberator!" The tone in which he was thus addressed was one of profound gratitude and tremendous respect. Within days, I began to be introduced as "Daughter of a Liberator," which made me feel both humble and a little embarrassed because I had done nothing to earn what was obviously a term of great honour. In each similar greeting was a palpable strengthening of the wartime links forged between Holland and Canada.

As I met the Apeldoorn Rotary Club members, Michiel stood beside me and whispered a brief fact about each person, who they were in the club, their business or occupation. After introducing me to one elderly man, who was somewhat stooped with age, Michiel said quietly, "That man was Prince Bernhard's secretary when the war broke out. When the Royal Family fled to Britain, he remained behind. After his arrest, when the Nazis found out who he was, they seemed to take particular delight in ill-treating him. I'm told that he is bent not entirely with age, but because of bones that were broken and not set properly." As I watched the man take his seat, Michiel added that the old gentleman knew the baroness who had escaped with Mona—but Michiel cautioned that the man was not anxious for me to re-open the subject of the war, and the baroness felt the same way. Michiel said there are a number of people, especially older ones, who consider the war a closed subject. It happened, it was dreadful, many people suffered, but it is all over, and discussing it brings only fresh pain.

After Michiel's introduction, I stood up to tell what I knew of

Mona and Willem Leonhardt's story, why I was on this quest and why, although I was a guest in their country, I would risk offending those toward whom I wished no offence. Terrible as the war might have been for some of those present, I said, and although I could never begin to appreciate what had been lost or suffered, those experiences did not belong to those who had endured them. They are part of history, and as such, must be discussed if there is ever to be any hope for change. I risked adding that, if Holland had been a child that had suffered such abuses, the last thing we would do was ask it to remain silent about what had happened. Instead, we would encourage that child to bring out into the light what it had endured, so that its scars could heal. Without sharing, even on a national and political scale, there is room for misunderstanding, hatred, and—worst of all—for a repetition of those original actions at another time, against another victim. I began to tremble as I concluded my address. But my conclusion was greeted with applause and many of the members rose from their seats. I was bold enough to cast a glance in the direction of Prince Bernhard's former secretary. Although he was applauding, he did not approach me as other members did, but rather he departed almost immediately. I was a little concerned about the effect my speech had on him, but I knew there was nothing I could do to take the words back, and consoled myself that it was better to have spoken from the heart rather than to have been mealy-mouthed.

The departure of Prince Bernhard's former secretary was followed a short time later by a message that Baroness Wendelien van Holthe tot Echten (whom Mona had known as Baroness van Boetzelaer when they escaped from the Nazis in March 1945) had invited me to telephone her. When at last I spoke with her later that evening, she asked why I was pursuing Mona's story, adding that she had spoken with two other writers in the past who had wanted to publish books about Mona. After she granted them interviews, she said, she never heard about the author or the project again. I condensed what I'd said at the Rotary Club earlier that evening, adding that I wanted to let Canadians know about the wartime role played by one of its female citizens—a rarity in Canadian history. Wendelien sighed, and said that the

war had happened a very long time ago, and that as much as she
didn't want to talk about it, she would see me if I returned to
Holland in the future. She was leaving the following morning for
a month in Switzerland. We set a tentative date to meet at her
home in Den Haag in July.

Vestiges of the devastation suffered by Holland during the war
were evident at our next stop in Amersfoort. Rotary Club member Rudi Bakker took us on a tour of a neighbourhood destroyed
by bombs and artillery during the war. Though rebuilt after the
war, it was done so in a particularly creative and haunting fashion. The area was divided into several sections, and architects
from around the world were invited to submit design proposals
for reconstruction, which started in the 1950s and continued
until just a few years ago. The ground plan combines quiet, narrow streets and wider avenues with original and manufactured
canals, along which stand uniquely-designed row houses.
Though none of it is lavish, no ticky-tacky boxes are to be found
here. Bombed-out houses that were burnt hulls at war's end have
been made habitable again. The facades were reinforced, and the
new houses built inside the shells—a living testament to remembrance. To avoid a potentially maudlin atmosphere, designers
incorporated little surprises—such as a Greek column or arch-
way—at intervals, rather like a smile. Though the overall effect
of the presence of those silent witnesses cannot be said to be
beautiful, it is certainly striking and entirely appropriate in a
country that suffered so much, and which rose again from the
ashes left by war.

The luncheon with the Amersfoort Rotary Club yielded two
small but significant pieces of information. One member offered
the name and address of Willem Leonhardt's nephew, Gustav, an
internationally-renowned musician and conductor, who has
written several books and who portrayed Johann Sebastian Bach
in a film of the composer's life. The second piece of information
came when I casually mentioned the name of Willem's business
(at the time, I knew nothing but the name). Rudi Bakker gleefully
said that he knew the company well. He had been in the same
business-plumbing fixtures and supplies—when Peck &

Company was bought by another around 1964. His information meshed with something Wendelien had said the night before; she had commented that Mona and Willem's bathroom had astounded her with its colour scheme—pink and purple—because such colours were not common in post-war Europe and she had surmised the fixtures could only have come from America. Small pieces of the story, but nonetheless important in constructing the background of Mona's life.

Two days later, Robbins and I were in Delft at the invitation of the local Rotary Club. Again, club members were warm, though much more informal than the first two clubs. Although no one could provide details or leads about Mona, they listened attentively and promised to pass on any information received. Our hosts that night were Eberhard Lange, a doctor, and his American-born wife, Monya, a publisher. Their home is a three-storey eighteenth-century residence which has been the office for numerous huis artz, or family practitioners, over the years. The term huis artz means literally house doctor, or doctor whose practice is in his home. The doctor from whom Eberhard had purchased his practice was still an active member of Rotary at age 91, though he had been unable to attend the meeting the day I was there because his wife was unwell. I was particularly disappointed not to have met him once Eberhard and Monya told me of his activities during World War Two. Although the doctor's story does not pertain directly to Mona's, it gives insight into the risks ordinary people were willing to take during the war, the sacrifices they made, and the consequences with which they had to live, or which cost them their lives.

Because this Delft doctor's practice was located in his house, it was ideal for resistance activities. Many people could pass through the office without raising suspicion, either from the Nazis or from those collaborating with them. Standing in the quiet back garden, through which a gate provides access to a quiet side street rather than to the busy main thoroughfare, it's easy to imagine the clandestine comings and goings that took place there in World War Two. However, after Holland had been occupied by the Nazis for a few years, any place with such free public access was bound to be watched more closely and to receive more unwelcome visits from Nazi officials. The doctor's house was no exception. After unsuccessful Nazi attempts to incite the Dutch to turn against their Jewish neighbours, workers and students retaliated by staging a general strike in February 1941. The Nazis had not expected the Dutch to be more reticent toward overt anti-Jewish policies than other nations had been, and they moved swiftly to make examples of key organizers. A number of university students in Delft were rounded up and imprisoned at Scheveningen, a popular resort town that also had a prison which quickly became known as the Oranje Hotel for the number of loyal Dutch incarcerated there. The citizens of Delft were informed that students would be released when more key players in the underground movement either came forward or were turned in. The doctor was one of those whom the Nazis hoped to get their hooks in, but the doctor was certain that the imprisoned students would not be released, even if he gave himself up. Many others who knew of the doctor's role kept silent. But nothing could comfort him or assuage his guilt when the students died before a firing squad on the beach at Scheveningen, though the doctor realized he could not save them. He carried this guilt for many years, convinced that people never really forgave him. However, when Eberhard took over the practice, he and Monya gave a farewell reception—and more than two thousand people turned out to wish the old doctor well.

That night I slept in the large attic room used as a hiding place during the war, and imagined that the rumblings of the nearby high-speed train that shook this solid, eighteenth-century edifice to its foundations were actually the sounds of World War Two bombs. I had to turn on the bedside light to calm myself down. I finally fell asleep, only to awaken terrified and confused a few hours later, when a thunderstorm let loose its fury directly over the house, again convincing me that bombs were falling.

A couple of days later, I visited Otterloo with Wim and Tonnie van Beek, who had billeted my father and his best friend, Warren Evans, at their home in Ede during the "Thank You Canada" bash in 1995. Some of the heaviest fighting took place at the National Park, and I imagined the calm greenness of its gates scarred by wartime activity, its birdsong obliterated by the bump

Mona and Willem lavished time and money in building "Ingleside," their home in Laren, North Holland, where they would later hide Allied airmen. *Top*: Mona with friends on the terrace (May 1939 or 1940). *Bottom*: the same view of the house today, now owned by Baron and Baroness van Heeckeren (May 1998).

Then and now: Mona's beloved Ingleside garden—seen in this 1940 postcard (*above*)—is remarkably unchanged, almost sixty years later.

of artillery and staccato machine gun fire; I could almost taste the dust and smoke as the peace of that place was torn up. In the centre of the town—razed in the war—new houses and an elementary school had risen from the rubble and ashes.

The day after our visit to Ede and Otterloo, Robbins and I made the trip we had looked forward to most of all: Ingleside. The home, named as a play on the Dutch word for English (Ingels), was built in Laren, Noord Holland in 1938 for Mona and Willem Leonhardt. Several months after our return to Canada, I learned that our visit occurred the day after the forty-first anniversary of Mona's departure. The owners of the house, Baron and Baroness van Heeckeren, invited us to visit, to see for ourselves the hiding place behind a bedroom wall, and the attic room in which two British flyers, Jock Moir and Richard Pape—the last two airmen the Leonhardts had been able to help—had stayed for six days in September 1941. Although given explicit directions to the house, we passed the driveway several times before discerning the lane that would lead us to the house, as though the entrance were still intent on guarding its secret from inquisitive passers-by. Hedges on either side of the drive shield it from houses built on what once was part of the Leonhardts' property, making the driveway seem narrower than it is. Flowerbeds nestle between the white, crushed stone and the hedges, the drive curving gently to the house, which is a large, white, stucco building, elegant despite its relative plainness. As the saying about books and their covers warns, the house's exterior gives little indication—beyond its size—of what is to be discovered within.

What was once the detached garage is now incorporated into the house, and a separate garage constructed opposite. We knocked on a heavy, wooden front door laced with wrought-iron hinges, pulls, and locks. The shrubbery, I later discovered, were planted by Mona in 1938, and the exterior light fixtures were also original. The van Heeckerens welcomed us graciously into the black-and-white, ceramic-tiled entrance hall; at the end of the hall the living room was visible—cosy despite its size, with a beamed ceiling and large fireplace, its walls painted in warm peach tones. A few large, heavy Dutch antiques accented the

room, much as they did when Mona lived there. The rest of the
furnishings were modern over-stuffed pieces grouped around a
granite-and-glass coffee table. Large windows, framed with floral
valances and drapes, welcomed the hazy sunlight. Two
Gainsborough-style paintings (though it wouldn't have been surprising to learn they were originals) graced the walls. Although
the house's interior was of tremendous interest, equally com-
pelling were the gardens that had meant so much to Mona. She'd
included one aerial photograph of her house and grounds in an
article she'd written for *Weekend Magazine* in 1960. After so
many years, significant changes could be not only anticipated,
but expected. But the only noticeable change was the addition of
a large in-ground swimming pool.

Despite the years and an interior decor that has changed since
Mona's tenure, I could easily imagine what unfolded that
September evening in 1941: Mona's feelings when she knew that
the Gestapo were at the door, the tense game waged for an hour
in that large room as Mona withstood a barrage of questions, and
the brusque intervention by one of the Gestapo officers as she
tried to leave the room to get her purse, after learning she would
have to accompany them to their Amsterdam headquarters.
There were the hollow echoes of the heavy front door slamming
behind Mona, followed by the roar of the staff car's engine fading
down the driveway as Mona was whisked away for nearly four
years of deprivation, humiliation, and abuse in Nazi prisons. My
flood of impressions was interrupted when Baron van Heeckeren
invited us to view a tiny room behind a bedroom closet, and the
attic in which at least two British flyers found refuge during
their escape from Nazi-occupied Holland.

Exiting the large living room and passing through the
Rembrandt-tiled entrance hall, we entered a smaller room with a
soaring ceiling that opened to the second floor. Halfway up the
stairs, I paused to look out a large, high window, and then gazed
back to the ground floor below. Something about the room
seemed wrong, though I couldn't place it. Later I learned that the
room had housed Mona's cherished piano, and that the oak-panelled wall had once been all window, to allow Mona a view of
her rose garden while she played the piano.

In a second-floor bedroom, closets spanned one wall. Baron van Heeckeren opened the door of the far left cupboard, which revealed shelves, both in the door and at the back of the closet, designed to hold shoes. He pulled forward the shelves at the back of the closet, revealing a plain white wall. A small latch, once tripped, let part of the wall swing aside to reveal a tiny room. The van Heeckerens used it for storage, but still inside was the narrow bench built under the sloping roof, a bench that could accommodate two or three people sitting, or one person lying down. Someone of average height could stand upright only against the interior wall. One naked bulb provided light, and there were no fresh air vents visible, so the space was not suitable as a long-term hiding spot. Likely the little room would only have been used if a search was imminent and escape impossible.

Back in the hallway was what appeared to be another closet door. It opened to reveal steep stairs leading to attic rooms, originally designed as servants' quarters. At the top of the stairs we turned left and followed a short hallway. Two doors on the left concealed a toilet and a sink. Beyond them was the door to the bedroom where Richard Pape and Jock Moir had slept. The room was large and surprisingly bright, with a window at either end providing air circulation, and allowing a clear view of the garden on one side of the house, and the driveway on the other. In his memoirs, Pape recalled that on pleasant days, he and Moir were able to leave their attic quarters and enjoy some fresh air in the garden, quite confident that they were shielded from observation by the small forest which surrounded the property.

Though the attic rooms were interesting, the garden below beckoned. Initially I thought the source of the garden's powerful draw was the fact that Mona had been an avid gardener. But once outside, there was something else—a feeling—that Mona was still very much a part of the garden. Judging by the one aerial photograph I had seen—postcards of which Baroness van Heeckeren had found when they moved into the house, and which she gave me—I realized the ground plan was almost as Mona had designed it 60 years earlier. The garden house, the pergola, and the terraces were in exactly the same place, although some modern renovations to the patio off the living room had slightly altered the appearance. It would be several months before I would discover photographs revealing that the area had been a terrace when Mona lived there, and that the bay-window extension was a recent addition. Baron van Heeckeren said the in-ground pool had been installed by previous owners some twenty years earlier, and that a sliver of the original property had been expropriated when the highway was expanded to four lanes.

It was still early spring, and many plants were only just start-ing to bloom. At one end of the garden, near the entrance to the pergola and closest to the house, was a large expanse of rhodo-dendrons planted by Mona 60 years earlier. Mona's delight and pride in those gardens are still palpable, and even a modest imagination can conjure images of her utter absorption as she supervised the gardener, pruned bushes, selected blooms for arrangements, and worked to rebuild the garden after its devasta-tion during the war.

As we left the house following our visit, I turned, on a whim, to take a photo of the front door; it was Mona's last glimpse of Ingleside when she was whisked away by the Gestapo, and it greeted her upon her return home nearly four years later. Several months after taking my photograph, I would find an almost identical photograph taken from the same spot, by Mona, 60 years before.

Chapter Three

"Gezellig!"

September 1, 1937 dawned bright, cloudless, and still. Everyone at Schoonord was up early to prepare for the morning's nuptials. Household staff burning the midnight oil in preparation for the big event hadn't been the only ones up late. Mona and Willem were night owls, but even after bidding Willem good night, Mona was too excited to sleep deeply. Her consolation when a chorus of birdsong awoke her early the next morning was that she did not have to attend to a single detail herself. Everything had been looked after by Willem and her future parents-in-law, and undertaken by the very capable Schoonord staff. Mona, with the help of her servant Gertrude, had only to look after Mona. First she indulged in a light breakfast of yoghurt and fresh fruit, then she set about readying herself for the wedding, setting her hair in curls and applying a face pack, and finally soaking in a hot bath delicately scented with the perfumes of the flowers she loved, and liberally laced with bubbles.

Shortly after breakfast, while the bride was still indulging in leisurely preparation, the rest of the wedding party assembled at Schoonord. Mona's brother Ross and his wife, Mary, were visiting from the United States, and were guests at the house; Norval had been ill and was unable to travel, so Ross attended in his place to give away the bride. Pancho and Marguerite Rodeweg were also part of the intimate group invited to attend the small ceremony. Pancho and Willem had been friends for many years, and were business associates. Marguerite and Mona shared an affinity not only for the good life, but also for a good joke, and they became close friends as the foursome enjoyed vacations together in the years before the outbreak of war. Willem's brother Georg and his wife, Trüdl, arrived with their three children, followed by Willem's maternal uncle and cousin. While everyone chatted and enjoyed coffee and pastries, the photographer arrived and began to set up his equipment. Upstairs, Mona was in the final stages of dressing in her wedding outfit: a cream-coloured, couturier-tailored suit highlighted by a short cape, topped by a saffron-brown fitted hat with veil, and leather bag, shoes, and gloves to match. In his room down the hall, Willem donned more traditional clothing: a grey morning suit, silk top hat, and white kid gloves.

Once dressed, Mona and Willem joined their guests downstairs. The women in the party were stylishly dressed, although Willem's mother, Victoire, chose a more conservative long gown with a short cape, echoing a slightly earlier era. Ross looked suave in his double-breasted suit, while Georg Sr., like his wife, chose more traditional garb—a three-piece suit. Georg Jr. and Pancho opted for dark business suits—entirely acceptable, by the etiquette of the day, for a morning wedding. Boutonnieres of ivory carnations to match Mona's wedding bouquet were distributed, causing some amusement among the women, whose attire lacked lapel buttonholes in which to place the flowers. Marguerite, who wore a dark silk dress with a contrasting, light-coloured, sleeveless over-jacket, gaily stuck her boutonniere in one of the upper central buttonholes that ran the length of her coat. Mary put hers in the waistband of her dark blue dress, and Victoire followed suit. Trüdl proclaimed herself more fortunate, and more practical, for having a lapel buttonhole in the dark overcoat that matched her dress. While the men congratulated themselves on having less complicated attire and affixed their boutonnieres, the limousines assembled outside Schoonord's main entrance to take the wedding party to the town hall in s'Graveland. In Holland, a civil ceremony was all that was required for a marriage to be legal—a church ceremony was

Mona and Willem's wedding at the town hall in s'Graveland. *Left*: Mona is flanked by brother Ross (*left*) and Willem (*right*); her father was unable to make the trip. *Below*: signing the register. Seated beside Willem are his parents.

The wedding reception at Schoonord. "Billy and I turned at the door—before entering—especially to have a good picture taken. This is the result."

optional. And, because the town hall could accommodate only a small number of people, Mona and Willem had carefully chosen those whom they wished to witness their nuptials: close relatives and dearest friends.

As they stepped out the front door, Victoire asked her son and his fiancée to stop and have the first photograph taken, marking their last portrait as single people. The pair indulged the request, although Willem, impatient to get things under way, muttered under his breath. Mona silenced him with a loving and gentle rebuke through pursed lips, but the shutter had barely clicked when Willem was in motion again, heading for the limousine where the driver stood ready to open the door. Theirs was the first car to depart Schoonord for the town hall. Behind them were Ross and Mary, who travelled with Victoire and Georg Sr. Then came Georg and Trüdl with their family, followed by Pancho and Marguerite. Bringing up the rear were Willem's uncle and cousin. All the vehicles were chauffeur-driven, but— in contrast to the fleet of black limousines in which their friends and relations travelled—the car in which Mona and Willem rode was a soft green limousine with dark green trim and a convertible roof, which Mona and Willem had put down for the trip to the hall. Pulling away from Schoonord, Willem made a dry remark about the attention the entourage was attracting; Mona cast him a glance and broke into a smile. Neighbours had already assembled on the sidewalk near the house, ready to be the first to wave and wish the couple well.

Each limousine drew up to the town hall, its chauffeur bringing the vehicle to a stop precisely next to the carpet that had been rolled out down the stairs to the curb side. As the guests followed Mona and Willem into the building, the uniformed drivers parked the cars and waited until the wedding party and guests were ready to return to Schoonord.

Inside the town hall, everyone assembled in the tiny room where the ceremony was to take place. Heavy curtains had been drawn aside to let in the sunlight and the windows opened to welcome fresh air, though these weren't enough to dispel the predominant atmosphere of stuffy formality. Three rows of chairs were arranged before a table that was almost as long as the room was wide. Behind the rows of chairs, a large clock on the black marble mantle ticked off the seconds as people chatted quietly and took their seats, silently observed by the large oil portrait hanging over the fireplace. The town official performing the ceremony took his place on one side of the enormous table, empty but for the blue cloth covering it, a small vase of flowers and, on either side of centre, two silver trays which held the ink, sand, and blotter required for signing the official documents. Opposite the official, on the other side of the table, sat the wedding party: Ross and Mary Parsons, Mona and Willem, Victoire and Georg Sr. In the next rows sat the remaining guests. Without exception, every one—even the children—sat looking straight ahead. When guests conversed, they did so as if riding an elevator together; their eyes never wavered from the front of the room.

Although wedding ceremonies in most Western cultures are fairly consistent, language was a barrier in Mona and Willem's. Because the ceremony was conducted in Dutch, Willem prompted Mona whenever she had to give a response. While this was a source of mild amusement, the overbearing Dutch formality also made it something of a strain. The service was soon over and the signing began: first Georg Sr., then Willem and Mona, then Georg Jr. During the signing, however, the oppressive solemnity was too much for Mary, who turned toward Mona and quietly asked, given the language barrier, how one could be sure the rite just performed had been for a wedding and not a funeral. Marguerite heard the quiet comment and almost laughed out loud. Not wanting to let down her guard and act inappropriately on this day of all days, Mona focused on the signing. No music, no confetti or rice, no bells, no fanfare. Just what was required to do the job. The real party would start at Schoonord, where the Leonhardts were to be joined by a much larger group of family and friends.

Once back at Schoonord, there was one more ritual to be performed, and the household staff turned out at the entrance to witness it. The children were given baskets of rose petals, which they scattered on the ground just outside the front entrance and on the steps leading into the house. The newlyweds were the first to walk over the petals and enter the house, stopping to shake the hand and accept the good wishes of each servant as they did so. Their family and guests followed them through the house to the large terrace, where delicacies had been laid out on tables covered with crisp white linen and placed under awnings to protect the food from the sun. Next to the food stood rows of champagne glasses, which were quickly charged with vintage bubbly and distributed to guests. The first toast was made by Mona and Willem to each other's "first health," quickly followed by toasts from Victoire and Georg Sr. Victoire declared her pleasure at having another woman in the family, and Georg complimented his son's taste in his selection of a bride. Mona was thoroughly charmed and beamed her appreciation to both.

One of the guests who attended the garden reception was Lie van Oldenborgh, who, with her husband, was an old friend of Willem's. Dressed in a floral, two-piece suit with wide-brimmed white hat, diminutive Lie raised her glass and smiled as Mona and Willem toasted one another. When she met Mona just a few weeks earlier, she wasn't sure how well the vivacious North American would take to the formality and reserve of upper-class European society. Mona was neither uncultured nor unsophisticated, but even her broad experiences in North America could not have prepared her for what greeted her in Holland. The affluent Leonhardt family had lived in the Netherlands since the eighteenth century, after emigrating from Germany, and while they weren't of the oldest lineage, they had established themselves as a respectable, almost venerated, business family. In the brief time leading up to her marriage to Willem, Mona had seen more reserve than she'd ever thought possible, from the distinction between classes, to the formal way in which family members greeted one another. Mona had shared with Lie some of her dismay and amusement at the protocols and formalities she'd encountered. Lie, who spoke English well, marvelled at Mona's ability to adapt to life in a country that was not only far from her home and everything she found familiar, but one where she did not speak the language. That was not insignificant, considering that few Dutch could speak English in those days. Holland was an isolated country, without the cosmopolitan face it has today. If the formality and customs of her new country were a shock to Mona, she never let on. The easy grace for which so many remembered her back home was precisely what helped her ease into the patterns and routines of her new country.

Another guest at the Leonhardts' wedding reception was Pam Houtappels, and she, too, was an old friend of Willem's, though not one of whom his parents entirely approved—at least, not as a prospective marriage partner. Pam and Willem's friendship would take on more intimate overtones when the two became lovers—or perhaps rekindled an old passion that had lain dormant for some years—in the next two years. But on September 1, 1937, Pam joined the well-wishers in toasting the health and happiness of the newlyweds. That day there was no hint of difficulties, jealousies, or of the far more dramatic and harrowing events to come. Just a beautiful, sunny day, lots of good food, excellent drink, and family and friends to share it all—truly what the Dutch call *gezellig*.

For their honeymoon, Mona and Willem packed their bags, hopped into Willem's light-green Jaguar and took an extended trip through Europe toward the French and Italian Rivieras, with stops in Orange, Cap Martin, Nice, Cannes, Marseilles, Avignon, Ascona, Torino, and Monte Carlo. Mona sent pictures back to Canada of she and her new husband drinking Chianti during a picnic by a river in France ("It's not safe to drink water in those countries," she playfully assured family back home). In Orange, they visited one of the most spectacularly-preserved Roman theatres in existence. The stage in the ruins created a nexus for Mona's passion for theatre and her rich imagination. She savoured the thought of what it might have been like to act on that stage before a packed house, and then just as quickly saw herself in the audience, witnessing some early performances of what would become classics of world theatre. Connected to the theatre by a small passageway was an arena where people had battled for their lives against wild animals. It made her shudder to think that so little had separated art from pitiless bloodlust—a thought that would resonate during the war years as she was reminded how small and ill-defined is the territory between civility and savagery, compassion and cruelty.

Not far from the Roman theatre, she saw a small, Roman triumphal arch and captured it on film. Over the course of several

Mona and Billy honeymoon on the French and Italian riviera. *Above*: The couple relax in front of the bathhouses at Cap Martin, France.

Above: "Billy and Me on a wall overlooking the sweet little fishing village of Portofino, Italia." *Centre:* Mona poses on the running board of their Jaguar, on the road from Monte Carlo to Cannes.

days, Mona saw places that she'd read about or learned songs about, but had never expected to see, like the bridge at Avignon. There were ruins, aqueducts, and other vestiges of antiquity. Almost as good as Mona's sheer delight with all she was seeing was Willem's deep satisfaction with his wife's enjoyment. And there were other attractions, of more recent and popular vintage for Mona's appreciation and enjoyment: basking on the Italian Riviera, and staying in hotels frequented by the Duke and Duchess of Windsor, to name but two. Despite their happiness, the Leonhardts encountered subtle foreshadowings of events that would shake Europe and the rest of the world before too long. One such movement lurks in a photo Mona snapped from the balcony of her hotel in Cap Martin, showing a submarine just off the coast and visible in the blue waters of the Mediterranean.

While leisurely making their way home via Switzerland and Germany, the Leonhardts discussed where in Holland they would find or build a permanent residence—a conversation that had started not long after Mona arrived in Holland and continued while Willem showed her around her adopted landscape. They didn't want to live at Schoonord for too long, but neither did they want to rush into buying a house. Mona wasn't familiar enough with Holland to know where she wanted to live, but she was willing to trust Willem's guidance in making a decision. They had to be fairly close to Amsterdam, because that was where Willem had his office. But they also wanted to be close to family and friends. They discussed the merits of building a new house over buying an old one, and both favoured the idea of designing, with the guidance of a good architect, every detail of their first house.

By the time they arrived at Schoonord in late autumn, most of the flowering plants on the grounds had been uprooted, placed in pots and consigned to the greenhouse for the winter. Deciduous trees had started to lose their foliage, without the same extravagant show of colour that Mona so loved about the Canadian autumn. But there was still lots of green to be found, and the canvas on which Mona and Willem could imagine their own home wasn't entirely blank when they began to look at building lots in the area. They made their task easier by deciding

The first years of the Leonhardt's marriage were set against the background of the growing fascist shadow cast over Europe, led by these two men: Italy's Benito Mussolini (*left*) and Germany's Adolf Hitler.

not to stray too far from s'Graveland, finally settling on Laren, a community of just 3,500 people.

Part of Laren's appeal, at least for Mona, was that it vaguely reminded her of Wolfville, both in size and in the stateliness of its homes. Perhaps more important, Laren was inhabited by affluent young people who were less formally inclined than their parents' generation. And the town attracted artists and creative types, which Mona found appealing. Though the atmosphere wasn't bohemian, it was a relaxed place where Mona could be her own person and more at home. The Leonhardts soon found a building lot which, to those without much imagination, wasn't more than a mound—albeit an extensive, impressive mound—of earth, with barely any greenery. Mona was ecstatic about the possibilities, and as she bubbled about what she imagined on the site, Willem knew they'd found the place to build their dream home. Always a cautious, methodical planner, he derived immense pleasure from the energy with which Mona, her eyes glittering and her arms making sweeping gestures, dreamed aloud what would appear on the lot. She wasn't so much preoccupied with the appearance of the house as she was with the way the gardens and landscaping would take shape. As she described to him where the tea garden and the informal English rose garden would be placed, Willem reminded her that they were building a house in Holland, not England. Afternoon tea was an English tradition, not a Dutch one. Rose gardens and informal gardens with sunbasking benches were English phenomena, he teased, which might raise eyebrows and perhaps even ire in Holland. Without breaking stride, she announced enthusiastically that she had hit upon the name of their new home: Ingleside. Mona loved language, puns, and plays on words, and Ingleside was a wonderful play on the Dutch word for English.

Willem already had in mind an architect to create their dream home: Dirk Brouwer, an Amsterdam friend and business associate. Plans were quickly created and approved because the Leonhardts had a precise idea of what they wanted, and Brouwer was able to translate their dreams into technical drawings. The building process was further expedited by the mild Dutch winters, so excavations for the house began as soon as final drawings were approved and a builder found. Construction continued with little interruption throughout the winter. Like most Dutch houses, Ingleside had no basement. Once the concrete slab was in place, the shell rose quickly, outlining generous living quarters on two floors, plus servants' quarters in the full attic. Mona visited the building site almost daily, if only for a quick glance at the progress. The rest of the time she was occupied with purchasing and planning the details of the house's interior and gardens. Invaluable in this whole process was their chauffeur, named de Boer. Willem's firm provided the services of the chauffeur, who became a godsend for Mona because de Boer could not only speak English fluently and therefore act as her translator, he could take her wherever she needed to go to find exactly what she wanted for the house. By the spring of 1938, the Leonhardts' home at 7 Plein was ready for them to take possession, and a small household staff (including a gardener) was hired to help get things off to a smooth start. De Boer continued to serve as chauffeur, but did not require quarters at Ingleside as he and his family lived close by.

When the house was completed, Mona and Willem commissioned a commemorative "1938" in ironwork to be placed on the exterior of the house's main chimney. Because their priority was the house's interior, the Leonhardts had planned the exterior landscaping in stages. They got started that first summer, and planted spring bulbs that autumn. Shrubs and trees were ordered and planted, enhanced with further additions over the next two years. In order to achieve the effect she desired, Mona drew on all her expertise to combine fast-growing varieties with those that required longer growing periods. She spent a significant part of her first winter at Ingleside staring out at the garden's winter landscape and contemplating, over cups of hot tea, how it would grow and change in the following year. Each trip she and Willem took in Europe, Mona took careful note of plant varieties that she found unusual or attractive as possible additions to her Ingleside gardens.

Not long after the Leonhardts moved in to Ingleside, the weather was sufficiently warm for Mona to order breakfast to be

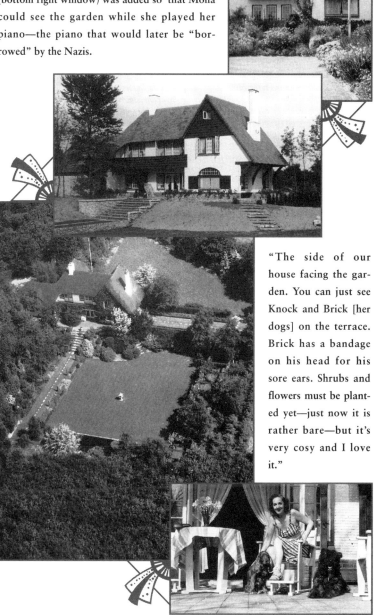

Ingleside 1937—1938. *Right*: The large window (bottom right window) was added so that Mona could see the garden while she played her piano—the piano that would later be "borrowed" by the Nazis.

"The side of our house facing the garden. You can just see Knock and Brick [her dogs] on the terrace. Brick has a bandage on his head for his sore ears. Shrubs and flowers must be planted yet—just now it is rather bare—but it's very cosy and I love it."

served on the terrace. Willem had already left for work, but Mona didn't mind having the first terrace breakfast on her own. In fact, she was rather happy to be alone to drink in the warmth and brilliance of the sun. Although Mona had enjoyed the sun's heat on the Riviera, this little ritual was a particular pleasure that hearkened back to childhood, back to the Annapolis Valley, to the end of winter, when skin made almost impervious to warmth by winter's chill suddenly felt new heat gathering in the sun's rays. A simple pleasure, and a Canadian one as distinctive as the first time she stepped out of doors on an early spring day, and noticed she could smell earth—earth that would soon be warm enough to yield more than crocuses and snowdrops. The experience was one that Mona all but forgot until the next time it happened, and one that had been with her as long as she could remember, marking many transitions in her life besides the one from winter to spring. Her need to feel these sensations would be heightened in a few short years, when imprisonment would make even more precious the rare opportunities when she was allowed such simple moments—and when her appreciation of them was even more meaningful. Later that first day, she ventured to take afternoon tea in the new tea nook, a small patio furnished with chairs, a table and a loveseat made from tree boughs, and a sunbasking bench made of concrete and covered with upholstered padding. The area was surrounded on three sides with hedgerow to provide a wind break, but that first spring day the shrubbery was still short, so Mona donned a light sweater. She was comforted when she detected the sun working its way through the fibres to warm her skin beneath. Only a few more weeks, she told herself, and the sun would be powerful enough to entice her to wear only a bathing costume. She began to count the days as she closed her eyes and savoured the warmth of the sun on her face.

While the garden was Mona's pride and joy, she also brought careful attention to Ingleside's interior. Mona preferred clean, simple designs to serve as the basis for her home's decor. Flowers, ruffles, and frills were not her style, but she appreciated the artistry in Willem's heavy, Dutch antiques. She used these carefully and tastefully as accent pieces in various parts of the house—large wardrobes in each of their private dressing rooms, a chest of drawers and heavy, bevelled mirror in the front entrance hall, and an exquisite dining room suite. But Mona's most treasured possession wasn't one of the antiques they owned, but a blond-oak baby grand piano, a gift from Willem. When they designed the house, they'd included a small conservatory with two-storey-high windows overlooking the rose gardens, so that Mona could gaze over them while playing the piano. And Mona used the piano for many of her different moods, to entertain friends who had gathered for dinner, to idly pick out tunes while she considered the next phase of her garden, and to play some of her favourite classical pieces on evenings when she felt restless and incapable of being contained by a book.

While the main floor of the house had been designed with guests and entertaining in mind, the second floor of the house was primarily dedicated to the Leonhardts' private use, and to their leisure and relaxation. Their bedroom was a spacious area occupying one end of the house, with a balcony overlooking the terrace and sunken garden at the back of the house. Off the master bedroom was a large bathroom decorated in sea-green, where Mona enjoyed leisurely soaks in the tub. Also adjoining the master bedroom were two large dressing rooms full of the latest fashions in clothing, footwear, and accessories. Mona had an extensive collection of gowns from some of the best-known European couturiers, many of which she kept to the end of her life. And, while Willem's wardrobe was certainly less flamboyant than Mona's, it was almost as extensive. Their living quarters were opulent. A large, high bed fulfilled the sleeping function, but the room was designed with more in mind. Mona could put her feet up on an ottoman and relax in a large, comfortable armchair while reading a book or magazine, or she could answer correspondence while seated at the desk by the balcony window. A Hollywood dream, perhaps, but all of it was used on a daily basis while the Leonhardts were in residence. Willem had to be up early each morning for the drive to his office in Amsterdam, and it was not unusual for him to return late from meetings. Mona, on the other hand, was more at leisure, and she thoroughly enjoyed rising late and having a breakfast tray delivered to her room with the morning papers.

Although Mona was capable of running a household on her own, she was not required to do so. Riek and Johannes, a married couple, provided all the services needed, and resided in the servants' quarters on the top floor of the house. Riek was butler and gardener, and Johannes was cook and housekeeper. Both spoke English. In 1939, the Leonhardts hired a 14-year-old houseboy, Joost (a pseudonym), to help out with general tasks around the house. Unlike Riek and Johannes, he did not live at Ingleside, and he spoke only Dutch.

Joost started work at 8:00 A.M., six-and-a-half days a week. On most weekdays, Willem rose early, breakfasted, and climbed into his chocolate-brown Bugatti (he'd traded in his green Jaguar in 1938) to head for the office in Amsterdam. One of Joost's first tasks was to walk the dogs, Knock (a six-year-old Bouvier, and a guard dog) and Brick (a brown spaniel). On mornings when Mona rose late and had a breakfast tray delivered to her room, Joost delivered the dogs to her room for a visit before she bathed and dressed for the day. Between 11:30 A.M. and noon, Mona was ready to start her day, which might include some shopping, a little gardening, or supervising preparations for an evening of entertaining friends. While Mona was away from the house, assigning tasks to Joost was the responsibility of Riek and Johannes. By 7:30 P.M. he was in the garage, waiting for a familiar signal (three quick blasts on the Bugatti's horn), at which he'd open the garage doors for Willem to guide the automobile inside. After Willem went into the house to join Mona for cocktails before dinner, Joost had to clean the car in readiness for the next morning—a task he enjoyed immensely.

Although Mona was known for her casual spontaneity, she adhered to some degree of formality when dealing with servants. Joost (now in his seventies) recalls that if summoned inside from an outdoor task, he was mindful to remove his cap and clasp it in front of him. He was careful, too, never to thrust his hands in his pockets while speaking with the man or lady of the house. Learning how to behave properly was certain to put him in line for better jobs as he grew older, so he made sure he followed these lessons in etiquette. One of his duties at Ingleside included setting up tables in the great room of the house and preparing the bar, prior to guests' arrival for Thursday night bridge parties. During his employment with the Leonhardts, he learned the bartending basics necessary to cater to the tastes of the their sophisticated friends, discovering the difference between glasses used for whiskey and sherry, or cocktails and Genevers. Although the boy's day didn't end until 11 o'clock five nights of the week, Thursday nights were lucrative. These were the nights when he could supplement the ƒ4.50 he earned each week with tips left by guests. At the end of the evening, Willem added up the change left on the plate put out for that purpose, and then divided it equally among the maid, the butler, and the houseboy. If the amount wasn't equally divisible by three, the Leonhardts would make it up. The houseboy was also allowed to keep the small change made on bottle returns.

Mona and Willem's circle of friends were as likely to enjoy an evening on the town (dining and dancing at the Carlton Hotel on the Vijzelstraat in Amsterdam was a favourite choice for the Leonhardts) as a quieter evening's entertainment at someone's home. Both Mona and Willem delighted in the jazz and dance music popular in the 1930s, in contrast to the classical tastes of other members of the Leonhardt family. Often Pancho and Marguerite would join Mona and Willem on evening forays to Amsterdam, perhaps because neither couple had to worry about children. And, while Pancho and Marguerite were frequently among those who joined in small parties at Ingleside, other regulars included Georg and Trüdl, Lie van Oldenborgh and her husband, and, in the early days, Pam Houtappels. Sundays were usually reserved for quiet visits with Willem's parents, either for a midday meal at Schoonord, or tea at Ingleside.

Mona made an indelible impression on young Joost, who remembers his employer as a solitary woman, though not lonely or sad. He was impressed by Mona's love for and careful attention to her garden, as well as her pride in the house, and he felt that Mona enjoyed the opportunity to focus quietly on household tasks and projects. The entire house was decorated in the latest and most tasteful fashion of the period. Wooden floors were kept gleaming with careful polishing each day. Black scuff marks left by footwear often meant that Joost was on his hands and knees

1937-1938: Mona lived for one luxurious year in pre-war Europe. *Above left*: "Taken in Amsterdam after the wedding of one of Billy's friends. It is not good of Billy—but quite good of me, I think." *Above right*: "Billy—in Zürich with his new chocolate brown Bugatti. It's a dream."

Above left: Mona, Pancho Rodeweg, Billy, and Marguerite Rodeweg on the Italian Riviera. *Above right*: "Taken on my birthday in Zürich on my way to skate."

scrubbing away the blemishes. When Mona realized how much work this maintenance required, the Leonhardts purchased an electric floor polisher to make the chore less laborious and time-consuming.

The first two years of the Leonhardts' marriage were set against the background of the growing shadow cast over Europe by Nazi Germany. Like most of the world, the Leonhardts went about their daily lives, working, entertaining, and taking vacations. Mona and Willem travelled frequently on the continent, sometimes to take advantage of a private health clinic in Zürich created by Dr. Max Bircher-Benner. Both before and after the war, Mona and Willem made several visits to this clinic, which was situated on a large estate with several enormous and well-appointed buildings. Bircher-Benner had been a pioneer in the area of nutritional therapy in 1897, when he advocated that the path to good health wasn't simply through medicine, but through careful attention to both body and soul. The clinic diet consisted of fresh, raw fruits and vegetables, eaten with yoghurt and muesli. Meals were small and frequent, and while no meat was served at the clinic, Bircher-Benner created a diet which could be tailored for either the omnivore or vegan palate. Mona and Willem were so impressed with the results they achieved, they almost completely eliminated meat from their regular diet. Considering the lack of meat in Holland once the Nazis occupied the country, their choice was fortuitous.

But the Leonhardts' pre-war forays in Europe were not limited to spas and clinics. Their pursuit of health and happiness took them to the Italian and French Rivieras, often in the company of Pancho and Marguerite Rodeweg. They made the acquaintance of some colourful and fascinating people on their trips—an Italian marquis, an elderly and wealthy American woman named Madame Mordecai, a count or two, and other minor nobility. Mona, as always, was vivacious and charming, and she thoroughly enjoyed the company of European men, who elevated flirting to an art form. Willem didn't mind the attention other men lavished on his wife, partly because such behaviour was not out of place in places like France or Italy, partly because he was confident in his wife's fidelity, and partly because Mona obviously enjoyed it. Willem was more understated in the attention he paid Mona, but his affection is evident in one photograph, snapped at Portofino, in the way he looks at her while she is laughing at a joke we will never share, his arm resting on her shoulder. In another, taken in Cap Martin, they share a joke as they look into the camera's lens, and in the next, Willem captures Mona, biting into an apple and looking rather like Lucille Ball. Then there are photographs taken on the terrace of the opulent Savoia Hotel in Nervi, Italy, its lush green foliage, white patio furniture and large, striped umbrellas providing the backdrop for an afternoon with Swiss and Italian friends. Another photograph shows the women laughing and hugging Pancho as they said goodbye when he had to depart for Milan—another foreshadowing of a trip that Pancho would take to Italy in 1940, a trip that would be his last. But in 1938 and 1939, everyone was enjoying life to the fullest, sensing that it all might end on the morrow.

Chapter Four

"clues and leads"

Shortly after returning home from my first trip to Holland, I began planning my second, this time to meet Baroness Wendelien van Holthe tot Echten. After the frustration, blind alleys, and dead ends that marked my early research into Mona's life, pieces began to fall into place. I was contacted by Gustav Leonhardt, Willem's nephew, and my planned visit coincided with a break in his concert schedule. He agreed to meet and to share his memories of Mona and Willem. Hans de Vries at Rijksinstituut voor Oorlogsdocumentatie (RIOD—the Netherlands State Institute for War Documentation) eagerly began searching the archives for more information about the Leonhardts. Finally, Dr. Willem van Mourik of the Rotary Club in Laren e-mailed to say that he had interested a journalist, Marij van Donkelaar of the newspaper Dagblad Gooi en Eemlander, in Mona's story. Van Mourik thought that having a major article appear in a Dutch daily that served the broader area where Mona and Willem had once lived would be a good way to cast a broad net in my search for clues and leads.

Although the purpose of the trip was to research Mona's life in greater detail, my daughter Maeghan and I included a visit to Het Achterhuis (The Secret Annexe, described in The Diary of Anne Frank, which now houses the Anne Frank Museum). The exterior of the building is unremarkable and would easily escape notice, were it not for the signs marking what lies beyond the front door and the dark, brick exterior. How many other quiet, unassuming exteriors of similar buildings in Amsterdam had masked taut and desperate efforts to resist Nazi tyranny? The visit to Het Achterhuis helped set the stage for further research about Mona, knowing the activities that took place within coincided with the period in which Mona, Willem, and a network of others were helping Allied airmen. Walking through those rooms is a profoundly emotional experience, made all the more poignant the day of our visit when a little British boy of about four, climbing the stairs hidden behind the bookcase that leads to the hiding place above, asked in hushed tones, "Mummy, where is the little girl that's hiding here?" For a moment, it were as though Anne might pop her head around the top of the staircase and whisper, "I'm here!" Not a single visitor spoke above a whisper, as though to show respect for those who had tried to escape gross inhumanity by enduring the inhuman conditions of hiding there. Trying to imagine all those people living in silence in that small space for more than two years is almost impossible. Every square foot of that building is charged—perhaps partly from the memories of those who hid there and partly from the emotions of thousands who have quietly filed through in the years since it opened as a museum. The experience was reminiscent of walking through Mona's house, though the atmosphere at Het Achterhuis is hugely amplified. The exit is almost as eloquent as the experience inside. Again, no words are required. Opening the door and stepping outside to feel fresh air and sunshine on one's face is poignant and liberating. How different fresh air must have felt to Anne's face when she was dragged from Het Achterhuis, after she had longed for it, and imagined what it would be like to walk again outside, unafraid. And how must that air have felt on Mona's face when she realized she was finally free, even if not out of danger?

Gustav Leonhardt lives in one of the beautiful old canal houses gracing the banks of the Herengracht—once the prestigious eighteenth-century address for affluent merchants, and now home to the simply affluent. Gustav himself, slight and trim with grey hair, answered the heavy front door, revealing a marble entrance hall that ran the depth of the canalhouse. A curving staircase at the end of the hall swept up to a second floor landing and a small ballroom beyond. Gustav Leonhardt's home is more grand than opulent, but the man himself is quiet, unassuming, and understated. One wall of the ballroom is lined with multi-paned windows of old glass, through which one looks at a bubbled and wavy world beyond. At one end of the room stood a clavichord; at the other, a library table on which there sat a violin. Halfway in between, placed just in front of the windows, were two Empire chairs and an ottoman. And overhead, the entire ceiling had been painted with a pastoral scene. Gustav pointed out where the ceiling had leaked during a severe thunderstorm the night before; he was concerned that the painting, which had graced the ceiling since the shortly after the house was built in the late eighteenth century, might have sustained serious damage.

Gustav was ten when his Uncle Willem married Mona Parsons, a woman whose grace, glamour, and good looks made her seem like an American film star to young Gustav. Though she could take command of any room with just her physical presence, there was nothing affected about her. Instead, she was gracious, vivacious, and effusive, with none of the vulgarity a more refined European might expect in an American film star. Although the Leonhardt family was characterized by a relatively stiff formality next to Mona's easy spontaneity, his grandparents maintained a polite relationship with their son and his wife, visiting frequently.

Gustav remembers little about Mona's imprisonment, either in Holland or after her removal to Germany, but he recalled that his father visited her on a few occasions. Gustav's grandfather, Georg Sr., offered to pay a large sum to the authorities for Willem's release—to no avail. Gustav could not recall if a similar offer had been made on Mona's behalf, since she had been arrested three months before Willem. Although Mona and Willem corresponded with the family on a few occasions, Gustav could remember nothing about the nature or content of the letters, and no copies exist within the family.

The atmosphere at RIOD stands in sharp contrast to the welcoming air of Gustav Leonhardt's home. Though the archives themselves are protected by several security systems and measures, Hans de Vries is just as warm and helpful as Gustav Leonhardt. An archivist in his late forties, Hans wasn't even born by the time the war ended, but he is passionately interested in this period of his country's past. His energetic willingness to look for historical needles in haystacks is both reassuring and reminiscent of someone with an enthusiasm for detective novels and amateur sleuthing. He gently introduces visitors to the procedures and protocols of the archives: knapsacks must be stowed in lockers to prevent sensitive documents from disappearing. Some documents, in fact, are so sensitive that they are not permitted to be photocopied. Furthermore, some researchers are made to sign an affidavit agreeing not to publish certain items found in those documents. The names of the traitors, for instance, responsible for Mona and Willem's capture must not be printed; although the traitors themselves are now dead, two of the three key people had children who would still be alive. In order to keep them free from possible harassment or persecution, the identities of their parents cannot be revealed. But Hans is eager to be helpful, so he will let a visiting researcher know that though photocopying is forbidden, there are no regulations against copying information out in longhand. And so, armed with my rudimentary knowledge of German and a Dutch-German dictionary, I sat down to do just that.

The first file contained a thin booklet, much like an exercise book a child might use in school. Brown with age, it bore a serial number on the front, as well as words in German that identified it as a prison record book. On the first page of it is Mona's name, handwritten on a single line. After it came the terse recording of her trial date and of her transport to Germany. I stared for a long time at those few words on that bare page, feeling the intervening years slip away, and suddenly feeling as close to Mona as though a prison official had just recorded the information, as if Mona were standing in the room beside me. This was the first primary information I had gleaned about Mona-not someone's recollection, but a single item recorded at the time it occurred. It was as cold and impersonal as the regime that created the circumstances requiring her arrest and imprisonment. The next few pages offered more detailed information next to other prisoners' names, including death sentences carried out. The Nazis, Hans said later, became much better at record-keeping, because they acquired a lot more practice. And here was visual representation of that progress. Statements in other files were very detailed, and I began copying extensive excerpts by hand, not even stopping to consider who might be able to translate it all.

One fairly thick file was that of prisoner Jan Huese—a man who'd been involved in underground activities rescuing Allied airmen with Mona and Willem, and who'd been caught when the traitors' net closed around them. The file contained transcripts of the Nazi court's findings against Huese and several others in the network, as well as their sentences. The only mention of Willem Leonhardt was that he was still free at the time of the others' trial, and no mention was made of Mona, whom the Nazis were unable to implicate directly in the underground efforts until Willem's arrest. Huese was to serve a prison sentence for his crime against the Nazi regime, but he became ill with tuberculosis while in prison. There were letters from his wife to the prison doctor about Jan's condition, ranging from inquiries after Jan's progress to gratitude for the doctor's efforts on her husband's behalf. At the end, there was the doctor's description concerning the conditions and circumstances leading to Jan's death, followed by a startling prison infirmary photograph of him.

Wendelien van Holthe tot Echten's home in Wassenaar, near Den Haag, sits on a quiet street, set back somewhat and surrounded by lush landscaping that shields it from passers-by. Wendelien, as the house implies, likes privacy. That notwithstanding, she is a gracious host who ensures the comfort of a guest, even if the guest might ask questions in forbidden territory (how Wendelien became involved in the Resistance, her role in that organization, the circumstances leading to her capture and to the capture of her fiancé, and her fiancé's subsequent death by firing squad). Patiently, but with a finality not up for debate, she explains that she put the war and its memories into a cardboard box. Her activities during this period have never been discussed with her children. If they are curious about it after her death, then the box will give them answers. And if what they want to know isn't in the box, then they weren't meant to know. She has a 23-year-old granddaughter who might soften this resolve somewhat. In fact, she might already have had some success, because Wendelien gave a brief and tantalizing example of what will be found in the box: a magazine article written by Mona and published in 1960, in which Mona described meeting the baroness and escaping from the Nazi prison with her in March 1945. Despite Wendelien's reluctance to speak in depth about the war, she was good enough to describe what she could remember. And at the conclusion of our interview, she provided me with a copy of a tape-recorded interview that she had granted Mona's stepson, Tony Foster, in October 1985, just in case there were details she had not been able to remember.

Marij van Donkelaar was not yet six months old when Britain declared war on Germany. Her parents owned a grocery store in Delft, and her earliest memory is of being held in her mother's arms while standing on the top floor of the building in which her family lived, and which also housed the grocery business. It was a beautiful, sunny, spring day, but Marij's mother was crying and holding Marij so tightly that the child became alarmed. The only sound Marij can recall, besides her mother's weeping, is the drone of waves of planes overhead. When Marij recounted this story to her mother years later, her eyes filled with tears as she told Marij that the incident occurred on May 6, 1940, the day Germany invaded Holland. Another of Marij's early memories was of a man who came to live with her family when she was only three. She was told to call the man "uncle," but not to speak of his presence in the house to anyone outside. The old man was a Jew who had lost contact with both his wife and his son after trying to escape and hide from the Nazis. He taught Marij English nursery rhymes, but told her that she was never to repeat them outside the house (presumably because someone might question where a three-year-old was acquiring her English skills). Eventually, the old man was moved to another hiding place, and after the war he contacted Marij's family to thank them for their help. Sadly, he told them that his wife had not survived the war; his son contacted Marij in 1999. Such memories have propelled Marij to become involved as a journalist, doing research and attending hearings on behalf of Jews who were denied compensation due them following the war.

Marij was extremely enthusiastic about Mona's story, anxious to uncover as much information as possible. She intended to write a story for the Saturday edition of the paper, in order to reach as many people as possible in the area where Mona and Willem had lived. Marij told me to give her as much information as I could, regardless of how sketchy it was. I gave what dates I had, as well as the names of some of the people—Lee, Pab, and Anna—reported by a Canadian war correspondent to have been present when Mona returned home at the end of the war. I had only first names, and when Marij thought that Lee and Pab sounded "un-Dutch," she came up with several variations of Dutch names that might have been bastardized by a Canadian ear. When I returned to Canada, I sent her a photo of Mona to accompany the story. On the Monday after the article appeared, two people contacted Marij at the newspaper. One was a former houseboy who had been employed by the Leonhardts in 1938-39, and the other was a woman who told Marij, "I am Lie van Oldenborgh, the 'Lee' you are looking for. I was a friend of Mona Leonhardt, and was present the day she returned home, as the Canadian war correspondent described. I would like to meet Andria Hill and tell her what I know, but tell her that she had better hurry. I'm going to turn 93 soon!"

The Dutch military were unprepared and ill-equipped to resist the German invasion in 1940. *Right*: burning of the port city of Rotterdam, following an air raid in May of 1940.
Below: Amsterdam after a bombing raid.

Chapter Five

"the worst has happened"

On September 1, 1939, the Leonhardts' second wedding anniversary, Germany invaded Poland. Two days later, Britain declared war on Germany. Mona wrote to her father on September 4:

> Well, the worst has happened—and we sit by the radio constantly. Isn't it too dreadful. Billy is still ill—poor thing—and we are all most unhappy over world news. Of course, I don't go to Canada now. My place is here. Isn't it frightful about the Athenia. Do let us hear from you soon. I haven't had an English paper since last Thursday—and I only understand about half in the Dutch news—Sorry not to see you this autumn.

Although the Nazis determined a married woman's citizenship by her husband's nationality, Willem was concerned that if the Nazis invaded Holland, Mona would be persecuted because she had been born Canadian and was therefore a British subject. Mona had not taken out Dutch citizenship, but Willem was convinced that even this would not ease her way if the Nazis invaded. He bought her passage back to Canada in the autumn of 1939, but she cashed in the ticket, refusing to leave him. After Britain's declaration of war, he again urged her to leave, emphasizing that he loved her and was concerned for her safety. Despite Willem's purported affair with Pam Houtappels (which, if it occurred would have happened before the war) and despite any knowledge she had of his infidelity, Mona decided her place was with him regardless of risks created by politics and world affairs. With this decision, the Leonhardts waited to see what lot fate would cast them.

On May 5, 1940, Mona wrote to Norval and Alma in Halifax, telling them that she and Willem were fine, and that they were confident Holland would maintain neutrality in the war. She mailed the letter later that day. On the following day—May 6, 1940—the Nazis invaded Holland. For the Leonhardts, there was no changing their minds. The only option left was to let events unfold.

Norval Parsons tried desperately to contact Mona and Willem after the invasion, but his attempts were futile. In June, before Mona's letter of May 5 could reach Canada, their friend and business associate Pancho Rodeweg was able to get word to Norval Parsons via a company in Düsseldorf and Ross Parsons's company head office in Rhode Island, that Mona and Willem were unharmed in the invasion.

Because of the suddenness of the Nazi invasion and capitulation by the government (five days from start to finish), most Dutch citizens were left dazed and confused as the Nazis established control over the country. Many members of the military who had not been captured or killed went underground. The Dutch Royal Family fled to England, along with representatives of the major political parties, to establish a government in exile. As early as 1937, the government had begun to establish procedures in the event of occupation of the country by a foreign power. Unfortunately, the plan provided only guidelines, with no strict interpretation for government officials about their conduct in the event of occupation—whether they were to comply with the orders of their occupiers or proceed in a manner deemed in the best interests of the country's population.

In the early months of the occupation, the Nazis ruled as benignly as possible under the direction of a commissioner of the Reich, Arthur Seyss-Inquart, who knew he did not have sufficient German personnel with which to run the country, and so

Sept. 4, 1938: "the worst has happened." Until her arrest, Mona wrote frequent letters to her family in Wolfville—often through her brother Ross at the Nicholson File Company. *Top*: a postcard to her father written the day after war was declared. *Bottom*: "This is a rotten climate, but one can't get out of it this year." In occupied Holland, letters were censored (note the Nazi stamp) and Mona had to disguise news of her situation, as she does in this January 8, 1940 postcard.

invited the 11 general secretaries of the former Dutch adminis-
tration to stay on. Though each was overseen by a Nazi commissioner, the general secretaries saw their role as vital in carrying
out the government-in-exile's directive to maintain some input
in Dutch affairs—though by 1943 only three had the stomach to
remain in their posts. The only major change in the administra-
tion of Dutch society was in the police service, which underwent total reorganization and to whose strength was added
members from the NSB—the National Socialistische Beweging,
or pro-Nazi party. Even the Dutch justice system was virtually
unaltered by the occupation, with the most notable exception
being the dismissal of the Supreme Court president, L. E. Visser,
who was Jewish. The Nazis wished to convince the Dutch people that they were not enemies and that a union between the
glorious Third Reich and the predominantly Aryan-looking
Dutch nation would be a happy match. Despite these overtures,
and the fact that there were no historical reasons for hostility
between the two countries, most of the Dutch population resented the pro-Nazi stance of the NSB Party. When clerics from the
pulpits of almost every denomination in the Netherlands called
for the non-cooperation of Dutch citizens with the Nazi admin-
istration, people began resistance activities that ranged from
passive non-compliance with Nazi rules to more dangerous and
covert activities. It would be another two years before resistance
became a well-established and orchestrated network of people
and escape routes.

Britain had stood by helplessly while Holland was overrun by
invading Nazi forces, but when Allied airmen found themselves
stranded in Nazi-occupied Holland, there were Dutch stalwarts
ready to lend assistance with safe havens, clothing, food, false
identity papers, and a means of meeting Allied submarines off
the Dutch coast as an escape route back to England. Eventually,
the ocean route was cut off, and an elaborate escape network
through France, Belgium, and Spain would be created with the
assistance of groups such as Fiat Libertas and Luctor et Emergo.
But in the early days, prior to 1942, the contributions of many
individuals were essential in ensuring that stranded Allied personnel found a way back to England.

Shortly after the occupation of Holland, many of the Leonhardts' friends and acquaintances were approached to assist British intelligence or Allied airmen who were awaiting an opportunity to escape Holland. Mona's friend, Lie van Oldenborgh, recalled being asked discreetly if she and her husband might find room for an airman or two in their rambling old home (now a national historic site). But Lie was reluctant to place her young family in such jeopardy. "How could I?" she says now. "I had small children. I couldn't accept such risk." Still, she took what risk she could. "I wanted to help the airmen, so we gave food that we grew in our garden to help feed them. Even that brought severe penalties if caught. I did not want my children exposed to danger. Mona and Billy had no small children to worry about, so they could do a bit more than we could."

During the first year and a half of the occupation, Mona was able to keep in touch with family and friends back in North America, by sending mail care of her brother Ross's company, the Nicholson File Company. The head office was in Providence, Rhode Island, and because the United States was not yet involved in the war, mail continued to move between Holland and America quite easily. Once in Rhode Island, Mona's letters were forwarded by company officials to Canada. Her cards during this period are stamped with the Nazi swastika of the German censor, and the letter "C" of the Canadian. "Well and safe...we have been always at home," is how Mona describes their life, in a postcard written May 29, 1940; the postcard reached Norval Parsons after he'd already been contacted by the Leonhardts' friend, Pancho Rodeweg. "Our life is much the same as always," she continues. "We travel by bicycle always and it is very good for us, and the bicycle paths in Holland are lovely. Billy goes by bike, then by train to Amsterdam."

Although Mona assures her father that their life is "much the same as always," she probably included this to make sure her postcard would get by the Nazi censor. The fact that she makes a point of mentioning that they had to travel by bicycle "always" would not have raised any suspicion with the Nazi censor. But it's clear Mona is informing her father that all is not well. Prior to the war, the Leonhardts did not make a habit of travelling by bicycle.

Willem had to put the Bugatti on blocks, and resort to riding a bicycle to the train station to get to work. Still, they were far more fortunate than many, who were deprived even of their bicycles.

In a card dated January 19, 1941, Mona chats breezily about everyday things, such as her father-in-law's health, then suddenly she writes: "Sorry to tell you that Pancho Rodeweg died suddenly New Year's Eve in Italy. He was only thirty-eight. It is a great shock." Mona mentions nothing about the circumstances of his death, not even whether it was an accident or a sudden, brief illness. Her pointed failure to mention a cause of death leads one to suspect that Rodeweg met a suspicious and untimely death in fascist Italy. Nor does Mona mention Pancho's wife, Marguerite, in this letter—a woman who was a close friend, and someone for whom Mona would have been concerned.

Whenever Mona wrote to her family, she had to restrict her comments to family, health, and other matters that would get by the censors. In a few cards she apologizes that the long letters she wrote did not make it to Canada because the Nazi censors had turned them back. Because of censorship, Mona probably never tried to describe in her letters some of the events which occurred in Dutch society and which were challenges to Nazi authority. She didn't detail the dismissal of Jews from the Dutch civil service in November 1940; an action that prompted public demonstrations, including strikes by students at two Dutch universities. Tensions mounted, and Dutch Nazis were ordered to start riots against the Jews in all big cities. When Dutch Nazis were attacked during these riots and one was killed, retaliation was swift. Over four hundred Jewish men and boys were rounded up in a single weekend in Amsterdam's Jewish sector, and subjected to vicious treatment. In response, almost the entire working population of Amsterdam and its environs went on strike on February 25, 1941. The strike lasted two days and the Nazis used force to bring it to an end. Some participants were rounded up and sent to prison, and some were shot; others were deported to camps in Germany. Events like this began to wear down the morale of Dutch citizens like Mona and Willem, who were becoming desperate to see the conclusion of the occupation and the war.

Despite the war, life goes on. *Above*: Socializing on the terrace at Ingleside. Below: "The day Pancho left for Milano." Pancho Rodeweg would later disappear in fascist Italy, during the war.

In April, Mona was overjoyed to receive a long letter from her father and his wife. In her reply to Norval, she expressed her wish that she could see them, as well as Ross and Mary, whom she had not heard from in more than a year. She tells him that she's sending an entire set of photos, in postcard form, so they'll know the appearance of the house and grounds. "What a mess the whole world is in," she concludes, "everything is so difficult. When all is over we come to you at once." Showing signs of despair, she wrote to Alma the same day: "I'm fed up with this whole bloody mess—and living isn't much worthwhile any more. It gets worse every day. It will be a long time, I fear, before all is over and peaceful again. Would love to see you all."

In light of events in Dutch industry, business, and society, as well as the effect these had on the Leonhardts' lives, it's little wonder that Mona and Willem agreed to help Allied airmen. In fact, according to evidence given by Willem Leonhardt to RIOD in May 1946, they had agreed to become involved in helping the Allies almost from the time Holland was occupied by the Nazis—whatever form such assistance might take. Willem did not give specific details of his initial involvement with *illegale organisatie* other than to describe the final event which resulted in both his and Mona's capture. However, writing after the war, Mona filled in a few more details:

> Billy became active in the Underground, finding hide-outs for Allied airmen who had been shot down, getting clothing, food, and money for them. Our home was one of the hide-outs where airmen stayed for maybe a few hours or perhaps a night before going off somewhere else.

Willem's nephew, Gustav, mused that perhaps Mona and Willem became involved because they didn't fully appreciate the consequences of being caught, but the sentiments Mona expressed, though brief, in postcards to Canada, would indicate that she and Willem felt there was no other option but to help bring the war to a quicker conclusion using whatever methods available.

Chapter Six

"into the arms of the Gestapo"

Many friends and associates of the Leonhardts shared a strong desire to assist the Allies; one such friend was Dirk Brouwer, who was well placed for his efforts on behalf of the Allies. An established and renowned Amsterdam architect, the twice-married Brouwer was able to have contact with a variety of people without arousing suspicion. In fact, he went to great lengths to give the impression he was neutral when it came to Nazi rule. He not only convinced the Nazis that maintaining normal routines for his business was far more important than politics, he gave them the strong impression he was sympathetic to their cause. In this guise, he was able to give assistance to the Allies without detection—or so he fervently hoped.

In September 1941, Brouwer received one of many requests to help British airmen. This time there were two who needed to escape back to England. The plane that had carried navigator Richard Pape, flight engineer William "Jock" Moir and six other airmen had been shot down over Holland on September 8, 1941. One of the crew managed to parachute to safety, but the remaining seven crash-landed in a farmer's field near Zelham. Five of the crew fled, but Pape and Moir hid in a mound of hay until a farmer named Bernard Besselink, who had heard the plane go down, came to collect them before the Nazis arrived to investigate the crash. After being hidden by various people in the local area, the airmen were delivered on September 18 to Dirk

Brouwer's home at Emmalaan 10—a prestigious address near Amsterdam's famous Vondelpaark. Through Brouwer, the airmen received false identity papers, clothing, and shelter until their departure for England could be arranged.

Willem and Mona Leonhardt received an invitation to dine at the Brouwers' home on September 19. Dirk Brouwer used a carefully pre-arranged code on the telephone to alert the Leonhardts that this was not to be just a social occasion. The Leonhardts' car, which had been outfitted with a special gas reserve tank on the roof which allowed them to carry extra gasoline during the heavy rationing, was taken out of the garage for the trip to Amsterdam. The tone was something like that of a social occasion as the Leonhardts arrived and were introduced to the Brouwers' houseguests. After dinner, Pape and Moir departed with the Leonhardts to make the 45-minute drive from Amsterdam to Laren. Although they had to stop at several checkpoints, they passed through each without incident. Nazis were notoriously class-conscious, and the Leonhardts were visibly members of the upper class. Both the Leonhardts conducted themselves calmly, even exchanging pleasantries with guards at checkpoints. They'd had to pass through some of them frequently whether travelling by car or bicycle, and so were known, if not by name then certainly by sight, by most of the checkpoint officials. By the time of that particular dinner engagement with the Brouwers, the Leonhardts were able to pass through the checkpoints with only occasional verification of their identity papers. It was not unusual for them to have passengers in their car, so asking to see their papers was only a formality and rarely were the papers carefully scrutinized. Travelling with their British passengers late in the evening was also beneficial, when the darkness obscured the particulars of people in the back of the car, and when the late hour discouraged even the most polite conversation.

When they arrived back at Ingleside, the Leonhardts showed Moir and Pape their accommodations—the servants' quarters located on the top floor of their home. At this time, the Leonhardts had no live-in servants, and Bep, their housekeeper, had no reason to ascend the steep stairs which led to the attic.

The airmen's movements were limited as long as Bep was present—more to keep her involvement to a minimum if the Leonhardts' activities were ever discovered, than because of any aversion Bep felt about helping Allied flyers—but otherwise they had the full run of the house and surrounding gardens.

The attic rooms overlooked the driveway on one side of the house and the back gardens on the other, thereby giving them a view of any people or vehicles approaching the house, so the airmen were shown to an alternate hiding place—a more cramped and less airy room off one of the bedrooms—which they could use if they spotted trouble coming. The hiding spot was well concealed behind the back wall of one of the bedroom closets, which spanned the entire wall of the bedroom. The hidden room was located under the sloping roof, with a built-in bench that could double as a bunk for one person. On the wall opposite the bunk, it was possible for a person of average height to stand up. The room itself was big enough to accommodate up to three people at a squeeze. The only source of light in the room was a naked bulb and there was no vent to provide fresh air.

The attic accommodations of Ingleside were at the more luxurious end of the scale of those available to fleeing airmen; typical hiding spots ranged from haystacks to cellars. The airmen who stayed with the Leonhardts not only had comfortable beds and two large windows to provide light, air, and a view of approaches to the house, but they also had a private washroom, a radio and plenty of magazines to pass the time while awaiting an opportunity to leave Holland.

After Pape and Moir had stayed with the Leonhardts for six days, Willem told them early one morning that Dirk Brouwer had arrived with another associate, Willem Lenglet, to take them back to Amsterdam. While the airmen checked the attic one last time to make sure they had left no evidence of their visit, Willem prepared to go to his office in Amsterdam as he would on any other day during the war—by train. The airmen climbed into the Leonhardts' car, driven by Dirk Brouwer with Willem Lenglet in the front passenger seat, and made the trip back to Brouwer's home in Amsterdam. In a letter addressed to Officer Commanding, Holland office, 6801 - MIS X Detachment in

Wassenaar, Holland, dated May 8, 1946, former Warrant Officer
William "Jock" Moir recalled that drive:

> When we left the home of Mr. & Mrs. Leonhardt at Larne
> (sic) we overtook a German patrol car which was pro-
> ceeding along the same road to Amsterdam at a slow
> speed. They, I remember, "looked us over" as we
> passed....

But their car was not stopped, and they proceeded to Brouwer's
residence without incident. There, Moir and Pape were introduced to a driver, Pieter Nolte—one of several others involved in
the escape plan. Nolte, like Mona and Willem, was typical of the
people who risked their lives to save Allied airmen. Average people—not sharp-shooters, explosives experts, or masters of disguise—were those who helped. Ordinary people were willing to
take extraordinary risks, even if that only meant giving a stranger
a cup of tea, in order to help rid their country of Nazi tyranny.
Dirk Brouwer used telephone codes to communicate with some
people, like the Leonhardts, but other participants in their
intrigue frequently found themselves having to trust a complete
stranger simply on the advice of someone else (with whom they
may only have had a passing acquaintance) or on a gut instinct.
In the case of Pape and Moir, the assistance of several people
was enlisted to get the airmen out of Holland. But in this chain
of people, one man was introduced about whom none of the others knew anything—nor did they have the means to compare
notes with one another about this person. Instead, he simply
showed up at Nolte's home one day, claiming to know another of
Nolte's contacts, and presented him with the following note:
"The bearer of this note wishes to get in touch with the wild
ducks. I have the impression he is trustworthy."

    Nolte did as he was asked: he gave the names of the airmen
and where they could be found at Ingleside. Such was the degree
of trust and the need for keen instincts found in the infant Dutch
resistance network. The risk was to be expected. After Pape and
Moir left Ingleside, Nolte directed them to the home of a neighbour, Frederik Boessenkool, a teacher who was the next link in

this escape chain. The plan for the day of escape was to keep the two pilots moving all day, to as many places as possible, to prevent detection and capture by the Gestapo. The ultimate destination that day was the seaside town of Leiden, where the pilots were to be delivered to the home of a married couple, who would help them rendezvous with a British submarine under cover of night. Little did any of these men realize that this was a trap, and that one of the links in the chain was traitorous, as were the couple to whom the airmen would be entrusted. This same couple would ultimately be responsible for the capture of Willem Leonhardt.

But on September 26, 1941, there was no way for Brouwer and the Leonhardts to know that anything was amiss. As far as they were concerned, everything had gone smoothly the day before, and the two airmen were en route to England. Willem arrived at his office and went about his business for the day, while Mona tended to affairs at Ingleside. But things were to change radically that evening. At 9:30 that night, the Gestapo (or Sicherheitspolizei—SiPo, as they were known) swept down on the Boessenkools' home. Although Boessenkool, his wife and two children—the entire family—were taken in for questioning, they were released after the Gestapo made a thorough search of the house. But two days later, acting on new information provided by the traitors, the Gestapo again arrested Boessenkool. Word began to reach others involved in the group, some of whom made arrangements to go into hiding or to leave town. The Leonhardts tried to remain calm, assuring themselves that their participation had gone undetected. But they also knew that, if something went wrong, the circle would close rapidly around them. Willem decided to visit a cousin in Hengelo for a few days and avoid his office in Amsterdam, while Mona remained at home in the event of a visit from police. If asked about Willem's whereabouts, the couple agreed that the police would be told Willem was fishing in Friesland and was not expected to return for several days. This would provide the Leonhardts with sufficient warning to take other measures, if necessary—or so they thought.

Bothered by a toothache prior to the arrival of Pape and Moir at Ingleside, Mona had made an appointment to see her dentist

in Amsterdam on September 29. The tooth needed extensive
work, but the dentist was able to relieve the pain and fit her with
a temporary crown, and he set another appointment for the final
work to be completed that Thursday. After her visit to the dentist, she ran a few errands, returning home early in the evening.
As de Boer helped Mona carry packages into the house, they
were startled to find Dirk Brouwer lurking in the bushes near the
entrance. He informed Mona that he'd come to the house earlier
in the day to warn her that others had been rounded up, and that
she should join Willem in hiding. But on arriving at Ingleside,
the gardener had told Brouwer the Gestapo had already called
there. When the Gestapo had been informed that Mona had gone
to Amsterdam for the day, they said they would call again at the
house around 7:00 P.M.—now just minutes away.

Despite Brouwer's warning and his pleas for her to escape,
Mona felt no fear. On the contrary, she assured Brouwer, she was
concerned that if the Gestapo arrived and found her getting
ready to leave the house, she would arouse more suspicion than
if she simply awaited their arrival calmly. She told Brouwer to
leave as quickly as possible, and instructed de Boer to get a message to Willem, via Peck & Company, telling him what had happened and warning him not to risk returning to the house. She
was certain she could talk her way out of this, but just in case
she couldn't, there was no reason for Willem to arrive home and
walk into the arms of the Gestapo. Brouwer said a hasty—and as
it turned out, final—goodbye to Mona before disappearing
through the garden. De Boer went to convey the message to
Willem, leaving Mona to prepare for the arrival of the Gestapo.
With only a few minutes left, she tried to calm herself as though
about to step on stage for a performance. The only difference, she
thought, was that this would be the performance of her life.

Mona Parsons Leonhardt was a woman confident in her abilities. Those who remember her are unanimous in their praise of
her acting abilities. She believed she could answer whatever
questions the Gestapo had for her and dispel any suspicions. But
she underestimated her adversary. She knew there were risks
involved in assisting Allied airmen, but she had little notion of
the efficiency the Gestapo had gained during that first year of

Holland's occupation. She did not know the sinister ease with which the Nazis were infiltrating the early resistance, using interrogation and intimidation techniques that broke the spirits and the will of many people. Perhaps she was even a little idealistic, believing that nothing could induce a member of the network, even under the worst threat or interrogation, to reveal what he or she knew of the group's activities. If so, she made an almost fatal error.

When the Gestapo arrived at her front door, Mona behaved as though it was more a social call than an official visit. She feigned mild curiosity about their mission, invited them in, and offered them drinks and cigars. While they refused the first, they were happy to partake of Willem's excellent cigars. When they asked if Willem was at home, she told them the fishing-in-Friesland story, but their laughter convinced her they didn't buy it. Then they told her they had reason to believe that two British airmen had recently stayed at the Leonhardt residence. It was Mona's turn to laugh. She assured them that if any such men had stayed at her home, she would have known about it. The two Gestapo officers realized they were not going toe-to-toe with just any woman. Possibly they even settled down to enjoy the little game of cat and mouse for awhile. They demanded to see the rest of the house. Mona, loath to seem as though she was being ordered about, insisted they look around, because she knew they would find nothing. Of course, there was nothing to find. The game was now becoming tedious, and they played their final card. She was to accompany them to "the office in Amsterdam." At first, Mona was confused and told them that there would be no one at her husband's office at that hour of the evening. They clarified that they meant their headquarters, not Willem's office.

For the first time she felt uneasy. But she was not about to let the Gestapo know that. She excused herself to get her purse and a jacket, but they accompanied her, not letting her out of their sight. Then they escorted her to their car and whisked her away to Weteringschane Prison in Amsterdam. During the course of the Nazi occupation, Weteringschane gained an unpleasant reputation. A house of detention prior to the occupation, the Nazis continued to use it as a criminal facility, and also to house Dutch political prisoners opposed to the occupation. From Weteringschane, prisoners were frequently sent to trial, and afterwards either executed or transported to the Waalsdorpervlakte prison in Scheveningen (the infamous Oranje Hotel, where the university students of Delft were held before they were shot by firing squad), or to other prisons and camps in Holland.

Today, the skeleton of Weteringschane Prison still stands, located in one of the most lively sections of Amsterdam, famous for its street performers on the Leidseplein and the nearby Rijksmuseum, Staadgebouw Theatre, and diamond houses. After the war, the prison was closed down, and the space rented to artists looking for a painting studio or a writer's garret. After its use as an arts cooperative ended, the former prison was renovated and it re-opened recently as the Holland Casino, one of the sites and stopping points on the canal-boat tour and water-taxi routes. Sections of original exterior walls are still visible, poking up from the top of the new building like imprisoned wraiths, trying to escape—reminders of the building's wartime use. Today, the only thing a person risks losing upon entering these doors is money.

In September 1941, the stakes were much greater. Upon arriving at the prison, Mona was taken to a room for an interrogation that became something of a marathon. Though she was deprived of food and sleep, and relentlessly grilled with the same questions, she was able to maintain uniformity in her answers and feign ignorance on all charges, claiming she knew nothing of the people or the events to which they referred. Although she was terrified, she was also angry. The dislike of authority she had discovered in her youth was re-awakened. The harder they pushed, the more she resisted. As the pressure mounted, she became more reticent and emotionless.

At last, she was allowed to rest, briefly, on some straw-filled ticking on the floor of a solitary cell. When the interrogation resumed, Gestapo tactics changed. They appealed to her sensitivity as a woman of a privileged class. They reasoned that prison was no place for a woman of her sophistication and refinement. If she provided them with some names, they would allow her to return to her lovely home and her beautiful clothes. They explained that they had no quarrel with a woman like her—that they were just after the men. Furious at the patronizing tone of her interrogator, she maintained her facade of ignorance. The interrogating officer was enraged. Exploding with anger, he told her that he knew neither she nor her husband was innocent, and that it would be a matter of time before the necessary evidence against them was assembled. Brandishing a file that he claimed contained the rudiments of that evidence, he prepared to read some of it to her. At first, Mona thought this was another intimidation tactic, but what she heard shook her badly. The two British flyers whom she and Willem had sheltered had been caught in Leiden. Though Richard Pape made a desperate attempt to tear up his diary and code book and flush them down the toilet—and when pieces failed to flush, Pape scooped them out of the toilet and ate them as the Gestapo broke down the door—he neglected to exercise the same caution with one damning piece of evidence against Mona. In Pape's pocket was a card bearing Mona's name and address. On the reverse was the name of Victoria Tufts Pickett and the address in London where she was living at the time. Mona had asked Pape to contact Victoria, so that she could let Mona's father in Canada know she was all right. But Mona's message was never delivered, and the Gestapo acquired the evidence they needed to arrest, among others, Mona Parsons Leonhardt.

During her interrogation, Mona also learned that other members of the little network had been captured. Numb with shock, she listened as she heard the names of people she knew read aloud with others she didn't recognize: Bernard Besselink, a farmer; Jan Agterkamp, a journalist; Frederik Boessenkool, a teacher; Jan Huese, a businessman; Harmen van der Leek, a professor; and Dirk Brouwer. The thought briefly flickered in her mind that the Gestapo were lying, that the people named had not really been arrested, but that the Gestapo were hoping that upon hearing their names, she might betray something. But the cold terror that started in the pit of her stomach and rapidly engulfed her told her that this was not a Gestapo ruse, and that the arrests were all too true. She gave no outward sign of fear, instead feigning boredom at the unfamiliar names and offering incredulous chuckles when told of the alleged involvement of people she knew. She asked for a cigarette in a bid to buy time to calm her nerves. Lighting it, she inhaled deeply, and stared steadily at the interrogating officer. Calmly, she asked him why, if he thought he already knew so much, he was persisting in asking her questions. Her ploy worked. Angered at Mona's refusal to be intimidated, the officer ended the interview and tersely ordered that she be returned to her cell. A prisoner she might have been, but she was also a strong-willed woman. And her captors had to admit, even if not to her, a degree of grudging respect for her strength.

Emalaan 10, (*right*) former home of Dirk Brouwer, where the Leonhardts picked up airmen Richard Pape and Jock Moir in September 1941. Brouwer was executed in November 1941.

British airmen William "Jock" Moir (*left*) and Richard Pape were shot down over Holland on September 8, 1941. *Above*: the attic room of the Leonhardt's home (see highest window at left) where the airmen hid for six days, until they were smuggled out.

Chapter Seven

"gone was the young woman"

The night I returned home from my second trip to Holland, I sat down to listen to the tapes loaned to me by the baroness, tapes of her interview with others interested in Mona's story. As I listened to the tapes, I scribbled notes—Wendelien's memory of seeing Mona for the first time; Mona's attempts to smuggle food to other prisoners; the split-second decision to make a dash for freedom on that morning in March 1945. But one section on the tape nearly crackled with synchronicity, and sent a thrill through me that put the hair on the back of my neck on end. In it, Wendelien struggles to recall the names and locations of the two prisons used by the Nazis in Amsterdam during World War Two. Amstelveense Prison, she says, is still in use. But she cannot recall the name of the second, though she recalls the name of the two streets where it once stood. Wendelien slowly pronounces the street names on the tape in the hope that the effort will conjure the name of the prison. I found myself rushing to complete not only the names of the intersecting streets, but the name of the prison, as I leapt up—wrenching the portable tape player's earphones from my head—to grab my city map of Amsterdam. Sure enough, the hotel in which I had stayed was located on the street on which the Weteringschane Prison had once stood—the institution where Mona had spent the first three months of her long imprisonment. I had passed the site each day on my way to various interviews and appointments.

Because the publication of Marij's article in *Dagblad Gooi en Eemlander* in September 1998 had led to the discovery of the Leonhardts' former houseboy and their friend, Lie van Oldenborgh, I knew I would have to make a third trip to Holland, though I had no idea how I would afford it. Once again, my mother came to my rescue, and when I e-mailed Marij to tell her I'd be making another trip, she arranged for me to borrow a friend's flat for the week. That meant I had only to pay for train tickets, groceries, and a telephone card, so it seemed, once again, that the trip was meant to be.

At the beginning of October 1998, the fall issue of the Canadian history magazine *The Beaver* was published, and with it an article I had written about Mona. Within a few weeks, I'd received some letters from readers and was contacted by a Dutch-language newspaper on the west coast, which offered to print a condensed version of my article, in the hope there might be subscribers in Canada who held some pieces of the puzzle. And in early November, CBC Radio in Halifax asked if I'd record an interview for broadcast on a Remembrance Day programme.

The day the interview aired, the CBC received several phone calls. Most listeners called to express surprise—they were unaware of this Maritime and Canadian historical figure—and to ask for more specific details about the publication of this book. But two phone calls were of a different nature—and very exciting. The first was from Dr. Ron Stewart, the former Minister of Health for Nova Scotia. As he told me later, he had not been long out of bed when he switched on the radio and heard my interview. His alertness and wakefulness increased as he realized that he was familiar with the story. In fact, he was an intern in Los Angeles when he received the Acadia alumni newsletter bearing Mona's obituary in early 1977, and was so taken with her story that he had immediately set about trying to piece together the details of Mona's life. His search had taken him to many places (and to almost as many blind alleys as had my own pursuit of her), and he was anxious to share freely what he had collected.

The second generous and astounding offer came from Cathy MacRitchie. She and her husband had purchased a home in New Glasgow in 1990, and upon moving in, had found an old photo album in the attic. Though Cathy knew nothing of the people or places she saw in the album, she was captivated by the woman featured in many of the photographs, and whose script graced the backs of virtually all the photos. Backwards-slanting, the handwriting described the context of each photograph without painting the broader canvas on which the life of the subject played out. And that made her all the more fascinating to Cathy, who found she could not simply throw away the album. Even in photographs, Mona is appealing and dramatic—qualities that captivated Cathy MacRitchie, and helped ensure the survival of a pictorial archive of Mona's life.

When Cathy contacted me after the broadcast, she said she and her husband had sold the house in 1993 and had stored most of its contents in Cape Breton. Visions of leaking roofs on old barns and voracious rodents plagued me for an agonizing month. But the new year got off to a fabulous start when Cathy contacted me to say she had all the photos in her possession.

In the meantime, I'd received a phone call from another person in the New Glasgow area: Clyde MacDonald. He'd read my article in *The Beaver*, and called to say that he was related to Mona's stepmother. Clyde offered information he had gathered over the years, as well as the chance to scan letters and photos in his possession onto computer disks, for use in this book. Accordingly, I arranged to meet with Clyde at his home in New Glasgow on the same February day I planned to meet Cathy in Stellarton, just a few kilometres away.

By the time all this had unfolded so close to home, I'd already made my third trip to Holland, in November 1998, to meet and interview the houseboy, Joost, and Lie van Oldenborgh. Marij met me at Amsterdam's Schiphol airport, and accompanied me to the flat she'd arranged for me in Bussum. After dropping off my things and having a *kopje koffee* at the flat, we decided to bring each other up to date over dinner. I couldn't believe I was still on my feet when we finally said good night around 11 o'clock that night. I fell into bed and dropped immediately into a dreamless sleep. Allowing myself a period of relaxation to adjust to Dutch time, I spent the next day walking around Bussum. I wouldn't learn until a few months later that Bussum was the last

place in Holland in which Mona Parsons Leonhardt had lived,
prior to her departure for Canada in December 1957. She'd
resided at the Hotel Jan Tabak, a hotel still popular with the
upscale crowd. There I was, in November 1998, wandering the
streets of the same town that Mona had left in December 1957—
over 40 years before.

On Saturday, I walked to the train station in Bussum to meet
Marij. Together, we planned to take the train to Bilthoven, stopping in Utrecht for coffee and a brief walk around. We were to
meet Lie at 2:00 P.M. Lie, who was diminutive and spry in a
fashion that belied her 93 years, was waiting for us in the lobby
of her apartment building, in the company of two friends. She
briskly bid them goodbye, promising to meet up with them later,
and ushered us upstairs into her bright and spacious apartment.
While she prepared some coffee, she directed me to a bedroom
off the living room, where I found an open photo album on the
table. The first thing I saw was a portrait of Mona taken in 1938.
Up to that point, the only photo I had seen of Mona was the one
taken around 1920. Gone was the young woman who gazed
somewhere off-camera, leaving viewers to wonder who had captured her attention. Here there was a more mature woman in her
late thirties, her hair definitely more blonde than brunette, making eye contact with us, but still leaving us to wonder whether
those barely pursed lips meant amusement, slight exasperation,
or possibly even good-humoured defiance. On subsequent pages
were photos of the Leonhardts gathered with friends round a
table on the terrace of a house, The warm intimacy Mona and
Willem enjoyed with their friends is evident. In another, Mona
and Willem pose with their dogs in a way that clearly indicates
that, like other childless couples, they spoiled and pampered
their canine companions. There were later photographs, taken in
1962, of Mona and her second husband, Harry Foster.
Remarkably, Mona seems to have changed little. The warm,
charming smile still shines as it did in 1938, giving no indication
of wartime trials and abuses. In fact, she hardly seems to have
aged between photographs.

Although Lie spoke English extremely well, she frequently
lapsed into Dutch, and then always apologized for doing so.

Marij laughed and told Lie not to worry—my Dutch skills were improving and what I couldn't understand, Marij would elucidate. During our conversation, another valuable piece of information fell into place. Lie was able to tell us the names of those whom Marij had fished for in her article (Pab and Anna). At first, Lie thought Pab might be Pam Houtappels, with whom Willem had an affair. But after ruling out "Pab" as a possible bastardization of "Pam," Lie realized the name probably referred to Bep, the Leonhardts' faithful housekeeper. Although the Leonhardts' home had been occupied by Nazi officers, Bep had remained on site to prevent property damage and plundering. Bep had also helped Lie remove and hide articles from the house in anticipation of Mona and Willem's return. And Anna, Lie told us, was a young woman who frequently helped Bep with the housekeeping.

By the time we left Lie's apartment, light was already beginning to fade in the November sky. The night was crisp and a mist soon descended, leaving a hoarfrost on everything it touched, including our breath as we exhaled. Because the air was so still, Marij and I decided to walk back to the train station, but became so involved in discussing what we'd discovered during our visit with Lie that it was some time before we realized that we were walking away from the train station, rather than toward it. By the time we corrected our route and reached the station, we were chilled to the bone. I went to Marij's home, where I met her husband Fred, and gratefully devoured a hot, savoury meal he had prepared for us. By the time I returned to my flat in Bussum late that night, I was developing a cold. I got out of bed the next morning but went right back to it, in the hopes I would minimize the aches and pains. Reluctantly, I shelved plans to take the train to Amsterdam to peruse the photo archives at RIOD.

On Monday, I was well enough to keep my appointment at Marij's office, where I met Joost, the Leonhardts' former houseboy. After several years of frustration and blind alleys, I desperately wanted to believe that the people who had been roused by Marij's article to come forth with information about Mona were indeed telling the truth. But a streak of cynicism demanded that I retain some degree of jadedness when presented with the opportunity to meet these people face to face. Earlier remarkable coincidences notwithstanding, I felt that I had to retain some suspicion about Joost.

Any distance I was determined to maintain, or doubts about the veracity of this man's claim to having been in the Leonhardts' employ, vanished when he began sharing details of his employment with them, and when he produced New Year's cards that the Leonhardts had made from a photo of their new house. He mentioned some minor details that I'd gleaned from other sources, the sorts of details that someone fabricating a story would be unlikely to bother with (such as the make and colour of Willem's second car, and the almost adolescent male pride with which Willem treated the vehicle.) My budding Dutch skills received a real workout that day because the fellow spoke no English at all. Marij beamed her approval whenever I managed to accurately paraphrase something that had been said, and she helpfully translated whenever I looked hopelessly dumbfounded. The information he gave was particularly useful in providing a glimpse into the day-to-dayness of the early part of Mona and Willem's marriage. The man sitting across from me was 76 years old, but the memories he shared were those of a young boy. So, when he said that he thought Mona had been rather lonely, isolated by her inability to speak fluent Dutch, I realized that his perceptions belonged to that 14-year-old boy who still lived within him. Joost has now lived almost his entire lifetime, has married, raised a family, and proudly recounts that he is a self-made man who provided well, though not without hardship, for his wife and family. He has a much different appreciation for the Mona Leonhardt he observed in her privileged surroundings, and whom he later learned had been captured by the Nazis and jailed. He is proud in a working-man's philosophy sort of way, and inclined even now to believe that hard work and perseverance can surmount any obstacle. But when he speaks of Mona Leonhardt, his tone softens. He might have underestimated Mona as a member of a privileged class, but she gained his respect—almost reverence—for having withstood nearly four years of imprisonment by the Nazis.

Upon returning to Canada, I transcribed some of my handwritten notes onto computer. Other than that, I resolved to do little else because of Christmas preparations and a series of family birthdays in early December. The one thing I allowed myself to do was e-mail Cathy MacRitchie, reminding her to look for the photos she'd found in the attic of that New Glasgow home in 1990, telling her that I'd made a point of asking Santa Claus for nothing else for Christmas, so anxious was I to have the photos. Though Nova Scotia's winter had been exceptionally mild, the weather forecast called for freezing rain on the weekend my husband and I planned to go to New Glasgow to look at the photos and letters belonging to Clyde MacDonald, and to pick up those in Cathy MacRitchie's possession. Undaunted, we set out for New Glasgow. We arrived at Clyde's home late, but were rewarded by the photos and letters he had in his possession, and by the anecdotes he and his brother shared about Mona's visits to the area in the late 1940s and early 1950s. We left Clyde at around 5:00 P.M., intending to make a quick stop at Cathy's home in Stellarton before starting the long drive home to the Annapolis Valley.

Cathy greeted us at the door. Attached to her leg was her toddler, and in her hand were some papers it looked as though she had grabbed on her way to answer the door. She invited us in, though I was reluctant to accept because I knew it must have been close to the family's dinner hour. But Cathy insisted we accompany her to the living room, where she invited us to sit down. When Cathy handed me the bundle she held in her hands, I had no choice but to sit, because my knees buckled under me. What I had thought was just a bunch of paper turned out to be close to 200 photographs—almost each one with a note written by Mona on the back. Cathy knelt on the carpet and began laying out the pictures on the large coffee table in front of us. I tried to pick up a few, but my hands were shaking so badly that I felt silly. I had dreamed of, but never expected, such a rich photographic record of Mona's life. At the end of our brief meeting, soft-spoken Cathy simply said, "I'm so glad that her story is going to be told. You can keep the photos, but would you send me two or three when you're done so I can have a memento of her?"

Although research on the leads I found (or, more accurately, those that found me) was coming to a close by the spring of 1999, there were still a couple of remarkable coincidences in store for me in my search for Mona Parsons.

In April, I went to Ottawa to look at Canadian War Diaries stored at the National Archives, hoping to find some reference to Mona's encounter with the North Nova Scotia Highlanders. My accommodations were at the old Ottawa jail, now part of the International Hostelling Association. I'd stayed there more than 20 years before and, while it wasn't the Hilton, it was more than adequate for my needs. The only thing I hadn't counted on was the fact that, where my bunk 20 years earlier had been in the hallway on the floor where cells are located, bunks in 1999 were all inside former cells. Even if one were not claustrophobic, one might well have found the confines of a nineteenth-century jail cell a tad cosy.

After checking into the jail, I climbed the stairs to the second floor to survey my assigned cell from the wall opposite the door. There were no lights other than the dingy overhead fixture in the hallway, and even after my eyes had adjusted to the gloom, I had a hard time making out the interior of the cell. Stepping a little closer, I could discern that walls between three cells had been broken down to make one space large enough for two bunk beds on either side of the cell door, and four small lockers in between, stacked two on the bottom, two on the top. My confidence deserted me, and I retreated to the lockers by the stairwell door, where I rented storage for my backpack, deciding that a 12-hour day in the archives (and a couple of drinks with dinner) might put me in the mood for a bed in that tiny cell. During dinner, I reprimanded myself: Three nights in a small, dim cell were nothing in comparison to the nearly four years Mona endured in far worse conditions. I would be able to leave my cell at will, enjoy a hot shower, and indoor conveniences, and choose whatever I wished to eat and drink. I was far from suffering.

Despite this little lecture to myself, my courage wavered when I returning to the hostel around 10:00 that night. So I was thankful, upon reaching the second floor, to see a bare bulb shedding a little light in my cramped cell. Gratitude gave way to indignation upon discovering that the lower bunk opposite mine had been assigned to someone. Knowing that the hostel was far from full, I considered trudging downstairs to register my annoyance that staff had not assigned one person per cell until the number of people registered required us to double up. Then a quiet woman in her sixties ambled into the cell and apologized for taking up two of the lockers. I was once again relieved: not only was I not the oldest person there, but I had been paired with a demure-looking roommate. I assured her that all was fine, and she told me she'd walked around a good portion of Ottawa and had tired herself out. Originally from Glasgow and now living in Australia, she said she'd never been to Canada before; concerned that her wanderlust days would soon be over, she made *carpe diem* her motto and caught a plane to Canada. I told her that I was in Ottawa to do research on the wartime experiences of a Nova Scotia woman, in an effort to get more recognition for her sacrifices. Although we shared the cell for three nights, it didn't occur to me until the last night that we had not introduced ourselves. So I told her my name, and nearly fell off my bunk when she told me hers—Mona!

A final synchronicity in my search for Mona occurred in June 1999 at an awards dinner hosted by Dr. Ron Stewart at the Maritime Museum of the Atlantic. Normally I decline invitations to large events period, let alone those where I might not know anyone except the host. But this time, not only did I accept, I eagerly anticipated the event, in part because Ron is such a warm, generous person and I couldn't imagine him not putting together a wonderful evening. Upon arriving at the museum, I spotted the mayor of Wolfville, Bob Stead and his partner, Danny Chandler. We saw a few more people we recognized from Wolfville, and when it came time to find a table for dinner, we were joined by Bob and Danny. They had invited a couple whom they had just met, Gillian and Hugh Pullen, to join us at the table of eight, as well as another friend of theirs and her business partner. Striking up conversation with our party companions, Bob told Gillian that I was writing a book about a remarkable Wolfville woman named Mona Parsons. Gillian turned to me and said, "Oh really? I knew Mona. Her second husband, Harry Foster, was my cousin. In fact, she and Harry were married in my parents' back garden on Young Street." Gillian agreed to be interviewed for this book, sharing her memories of Mona from a period of which I had little information.

Chapter Eight

"enemies of the Reich"

Despite her immediate danger, Mona wondered whether any of her friends knew she had been arrested, whether they would be able to find her, and whether her message to Willem, warning him to stay away from Ingleside, had been received. She didn't have long to wonder about the answers to some of these questions. Lie van Oldenborgh was one of the first to learn of Mona's arrest. Although Lie had declined to give direct assistance to Allied airmen, due to her concern for her children's welfare, she spared no time in trying to assist her friend. She went to Den Haag to speak with a mutual friend who held a high post with the NSB—the pro-Nazi party—in the justice department. Though the man told Lie he was aware Mona Leonhardt had been taken prisoner, he added that there was nothing he could do for her. He explained that the Gestapo had damning evidence and that no one could intervene on Mona's behalf without inviting personal suspicion. Despite her pleas and arguments, Lie was unable to move the man. She confronted the painful realization that the bonds of friendship could readily be sacrificed for political belief, and out of fear. The only concession their former friend would offer was a pass that would admit Lie to Weteringschane Prison to see Mona. Lie accepted the offer and returned to Laren. She never saw the man again, and could learn nothing of his fate after the occupation ended.

Pleased she was going to see Mona, Lie maintained hope that some miracle would set her friend free. She prepared a small package to bring to Weteringschane: soap, biscuits, hand cream, handkerchiefs, a needle and thread, as well as a few articles of Mona's clothing. Composed, but holding tightly to her package, Lie was admitted through the prison doors. The package was carefully inspected, and then Lie was shown to a room where her visit with Mona would take place. A few minutes later, Mona was ushered into the room. The two women exchanged quiet, polite greetings, as though meeting for lunch in a fashionable Amsterdam restaurant, rather than a prison that was rapidly gaining notoriety.

"Mona was very calm, composed," remembers Lie. "She looked remarkably well-groomed and, considering the strain she was under, rather well-rested. We chatted as though we were sitting in her house—she was in command of the situation, it seemed to me. I gave her the small package and the clothing I had brought for her, and she was very touched by it. I can't remember how long we spoke with one another in that room, but eventually the guard told me I had to leave. Mona stood up, apparently oblivious to the guard as though it were her idea to end the visit. She came forward, took my hand, and thanked me for coming. It was all a bit unreal, until I realized that she had pressed something into the palm of my hand. Petrified that someone had seen this exchange, I murmured my goodbyes to Mona, who continued to look completely cool and collected. Not until I had gone a great distance from the prison did I dare to look at what she had put in my hand."

In Lie's hand were eight pieces of toilet paper (the stiff, coarse paper favoured by institutions until about 20 years ago). Mona had found a pencil and written a note to her friend, giving her a list of items that had to be removed from the Leonhardts' house: jewellery, papers, silver, and bottles of rare and vintage wine. Today we might be tempted to smile at the last item on the list. But to Mona, who was aware that many people had been turned out of their homes, only to have those homes occupied by Nazi officers and to have family heirlooms stolen or destroyed, the thought of Nazis living the high life at her expense was particularly galling. Even a small gesture like Mona's was of great psychological benefit. The Nazis might have taken away her liberty, but she could have the satisfaction of knowing they would not enjoy some of her most treasured possessions.

Within hours of Mona's arrest, Willem's brother Georg had dispatched a van from Peck & Company to Mona and Willem's house to remove some of the large furniture pieces and antiques. He knew Willem had gone into hiding and that it was doubtful Mona would be released as long as Willem was free. He also knew that he had a very limited window of time in which to act, and that he had to select family heirlooms that could be removed in the single trip he was already running a great risk to make. Georg, too, visited Mona in prison over the next few months; first, to let her know that her home was safe and that housekeeper Bep was standing her ground against Nazis who wanted to plunder what was left, and also to let her know that Willem's whereabouts were still unknown. Given the risks of talking while in prison, any references to Willem were cryptic during Mona and Georg's exchanges.

With assistance from Bep, Lie van Oldenborgh quietly slipped into the Leonhardt residence at number 7 Plein the evening of the same day she had visited Mona, and began to assemble the items on Mona's list. Lie, too, knew she had a very small window of time available to her, and that she could risk making only one such visit to the house. She had to be calm, and very thorough in her work. Once she was certain she had all she could salvage, she began transporting the items to her house, making several trips. The next step was wrapping everything in cloth and packing it in boxes. Once that was done, Lie and her husband buried the crates in their cellar and garden. Although outraged when Mona and Willem's home was occupied by Nazi officers soon after, the van Oldenborghs found some comfort in knowing they had played an important part in depriving the Nazis of at least some of the home's treasures and comforts.

In prison, Mona's personality gave her the ease she needed to befriend a guard, who smuggled books to her. Once out of solitary confinement, Mona was told she could send her laundry home from Weteringschane for Bep to wash and mend at Ingleside. Certain that Bep and friends on the outside would be looking for hidden messages, she sent some written on prison toilet paper and tucked in the pockets, hems or waistbands of clothing. Realizing the Gestapo would probably be looking for them too, she made her messages as innocuous as possible.

In one note, she remembered years later, she asked about her cat, Wimpy. A reply was concealed in the laundry when it was returned to her. Wimpy had returned home, then had run away twice. He was now staying with friends who were taking good care of him, and he was looking more like the lovely sleek cat he had been. Mona was delighted. Although she and Willem owned a spaniel and a Bouvier-des-Flandres—their second; Knock had died and been replaced with Brutus—they did not own a cat. Wimpy was one of Mona's pet names for her husband and the reply gave her the news she most wanted to hear: Willem was still managing to evade capture, though she had no idea of the details—that through his cousin in Hengelo, Willem had been given a hiding place at the home of an engineer by the name of Wilmink. Nor did she know that Willem had decided the best course was to escape to England, and assist with espionage training and activities there. Through Wilmink, Willem met Hendrik Gerritsen, a teacher and former reservist in the Dutch navy. He told Willem that through connections in the resistance, he could help Willem flee to England.

The Gestapo continued to detain Mona, partly because they weren't convinced she'd told them everything she knew, and partly in the hope that information might be smuggled to her. Even after other members of the network had been rounded up, the Gestapo continued to hold her at Weteringschane. Perhaps the Gestapo were concerned that a woman like Mona, whose defiance was now obvious to them, would not hesitate to resume activities with the resistance once released, and in fact would find her resolve against the Nazis increased. Perhaps they hoped to trick Willem Leonhardt out of hiding, or encourage him to give himself up in exchange for his wife's freedom. Even after the executions of Dirk Brouwer, Bernard Besselink, Jan Agterkamp, and Harmen van der Leek at Scheveningen on November 17, 1941, the Gestapo refused to let Mona Parsons Leonhardt go free. At the trial of these men, and a few others involved in trying to help Pape and Moir escape, the Nazi court made a strong statement that it would not tolerate even the most minor assistance to enemies of the Third Reich, stating, "When Dutchmen help English flyers to escape, they are helping England, the enemy of Germany."

Even those who had done nothing more than provide a place for the airmen to rest for half an hour, or a cup of tea, were handed sentences of five and six years in prison. The man who provided Pape, Moir, and countless others with false identity papers would, when caught, have the good fortune to be committed to a concentration camp, rather than the firing squad.

Whether as punishment, or as a way of encouraging her to reconsider her refusal to cooperate with authorities, the Gestapo sent Mona a variety of cellmates when she was not left to languish on her own. One pitiful soul of whom Mona spoke in later years was a girl of limited intelligence, who appeared to have been subjected to sexual abuse. Mona suspected the girl might have been a prostitute, although she was only 14 years old. The girl relished describing what Mona called "sexual depravities," although Mona never revealed the content of those conversations. Still, she felt compassion for the child. When Mona was told the girl was to be released, she gave her some of her own clothing to replace the girl's filthy rags.

Later, her cellmates were a Jewish woman and her young daughter. Because they were Jewish, they were fairly certain of the fate that awaited them, and Mona was inspired by their resolve to meet whatever lay ahead. Finally, Mona shared the cell with a young woman who seemed intent on helping Mona get a message to Willem—too intent, in fact. Mona's instincts told her not to believe the young woman's eagerness, and Mona relished the chance to use her acting skills once again to deceive the dupe. Mona told her that Willem was tall, "deliciously blond," and blue-eyed, when in fact he was of average height and had a dark complexion. After the young woman's release, the parade of cellmates stopped.

Although she was glad to be left alone, this sudden change in tactics perplexed Mona. She was uneasy, suspecting the Gestapo had found the information they wanted through other channels. Mona had no contacts on the outside who could inform her of the trap being laid for Willem. After several weeks of planning, inquiring, and arranging, Gerritsen at last went to Willem and told him that he had arranged passage to England, and it would cost between 500 and 600 guilders. Willem paid the fee, and set out with Gerritsen from Hengelo to Prinsen, where they spent the night. The next morning they left by train for Amersfoort, where they were met by a woman who claimed to be British, and two Dutch men at the train station café. One of the men, identified as Doornebos (an alias), would be their driver, while the other, Kramer, was in charge of the plan. The group set out for Den Haag, where Willem was scheduled to meet a British boat off the coast at Wassenaar.

Doornebos drove the group to a house at Beuningenstraat 10 in Den Haag. Kramer told them it was his house, and inside he showed them a British radio transmitter/receiver. He claimed to have arranged several successful escapes and to be in constant touch with British and Dutch officials in England. Afterwards, Doornebos took the car elsewhere, and Kramer, the woman, Willem and Gerritsen went for lunch at De Kroon on Statenlaan. During the meal, Gerritsen told Kramer that he wished to accompany Willem to the boat, if only to let Willem's cousin know he was on his way to England. Kramer said this could not be done, because the arrangements that had been made did not include Gerritsen's name. Gerritsen felt uneasy, but he could not insist. As originally planned, he left for Almelo immediately after the meal. The woman also departed, leaving Willem with Kramer. The two men returned to Kramer's flat, and shortly afterwards the telephone rang. Willem could not overhear any of what was said, but after hanging up, Kramer told him the driver would return at any moment and take them to the embarkation point. When Doornebos arrived, Kramer and Willem climbed into the car and headed for Wassenaar. At an underpass, the car was stopped by the Gestapo. Willem and Kramer were placed in handcuffs, and two Gestapo officers got in the car and ordered Doornebos to take them to the Binnenhof (the Parliament buildings, which had been taken over by the Nazis after the Dutch government fled to England.) At the Binnenhof, Willem was greeted by a Nazi official named Bläse with, "Ach, so,

Night-and-Fog Decree (Nacht-und-Nebel Erlass).

The Fuehrer and Supreme Commander of the Armed Forces

[stamp] SECRET

Directives for the prosecution of offences committed within the occupied territories against the German State or the occupying power, of December 7th, 1941.

Within the occupied territories, communistic elements and other circles hostile to Germany have increased their efforts against the German.State and the occupying powers since the Russian campaign started. The amount and the danger of these machinations oblige us to take severe measures as a determent. First of all the following directives are to be applied:

I. Within the occupied territories, the adequate punishment for offences committed against the German State or the occupying power which endanger their security or a state of readiness is on principle the death penalty.

II. The offences listed in paragraph I as a rule are to be dealt with in the occupied countries only if it is probable that sentence of death will be passed upon the offender, at least the principal offender, and if the trial and the execution can be completed in a very short time. Otherwise the offenders, at least the principal offenders, are to be taken to Germany.

III. Prisoners taken to Germany are subjected to military procedure only if particular military interests require this. In case German or foreign authorities inquire about such prisoners, they are to be told that they were arrested, but that the proceedings do not allow any further information.

IV. The Commanders in the occupied territories and the Court authorities within the framework of their jurisdiction, are personally responsible for the observance of this decree.

V. The Chief of the High Command of the Armed Forces determines in which occupied territories this decree is to be applied. He is authorized to explain and to issue executive orders and supplements. The Reich Minister of Justice will issue executive orders within his own jurisdiction.

A translation of Hitler's *Nacht und Nebel* ("night and fog") decree.

Leonhardt. Here you are!" The Nazi search was over, and the case against Mona and Willem Leonhardt finalized. It was December 21, 1941.

The present-day Binnenhof, the Dutch parliament buildings in The Hague, where the Leonhardt's fate was sealed by Nazi authorities in 1941.

Chapter Nine

"night and fog"

At 8 o'clock on the morning of December 22, 1941, the door of Mona's cell was flung open. She was ordered to dress quickly. In response to her predictable question, she was told that she was going to trial. Her resulting confusion compounded her initial panic at the unexpectedness of this news. Nothing was said about her husband. Her only recourse was to do as she was told and wait to see what happened. She wondered why, if she was going to trial, she had not been allowed to speak to a lawyer. She also wondered why, after almost three months of incarceration, she was being sent to trial so hastily.

Had Mona been aware of Hitler's *Nacht und Nebel* decree, her confusion might well have changed to terror. Just a couple of weeks before, on December 7, 1941, *Schutzstaffel* (*SS*) *Reichsführer* Heinrich Himmler had issued the decree on orders from Hitler. The Third Reich had come to realize that simply arresting underground or resistance workers had not deterred others from stepping in to take their places. The Nazis reasoned that the uncertainty resistance workers would experience upon discovering that some of their members had simply disappeared into the "night and fog" might create enough fear to dissuade them from further resistance activities:

"It is the will of the Führer that the measures taken against those who are guilty of offences against the Reich or against the occupation forces in occupied areas should be altered. The Führer is of the opinion that in such cases penal servitude or even a hard labour sentence for life will be regarded as a sign of weakness. An effective and lasting deterrent can be achieved only by the death penalty or by taking measures which will leave the family and the population uncertain as to the fate of the offender. Deportation to Germany serves this purpose."

But even without knowledge of the *Nacht und Nebel* decree, Mona's anxiety mounted when she was driven to the Carlton Hotel on Vijzelstraat—a place she associated with much happier times. Inside she was escorted to one of the ballrooms where she and Willem had frequently danced to the lively rhythms of popular tunes. There she was introduced to a young German officer who spoke neither Dutch nor English and was told he would be her legal defence. She objected that she spoke insufficient German to impart her side of the story, and within minutes another young officer was assigned to defend her. His English skills were hardly better than hers in German. But there was nothing she could do, no appeal to a higher authority, so she simply waited.

Although she was certain that the conclusion would not be in her favour, she tried to follow what was being said. She couldn't make out most of the words, but she did recognize that the prosecution was very hostile toward her. Writing after the war, Mona described the scene that greeted her inside the high-ceilinged, oak-panelled ballroom:

> The judge, a handsome, well set-up German professional army officer in his thirties, sat at the end of a long table at one end of this room and from the outset seemed to be fairly sympathetic toward me. To his right sat the *SS* prosecuting attorney, who was about the same age as the judge and typified the arrogant Nazi officer seen in Hollywood movies. He was a tall, repulsive man with cold, pale blue eyes, stringy, colourless hair, and heavy, thick glasses. He could have had a monocle. He seemed

so full of hate, I doubt if he was pleased even with himself. He appeared to have a grudge against the whole world and his immediate target was me. An aide sat beside him. My counsel sat at the side of the courtroom, to the judge's left. Half a dozen soldiers sat on one side of the room. On the other side were two rows of seats occupied by some *SS* women and others. I sat on a chair in the middle of the floor, facing the judge's table.

During the almost three months she had spent in detention, her diet had been poor—blue milk, black bread, tiny rations of mashed potatoes—so she found it difficult to muster the concentration required to follow the proceedings. Resigned to staring out a nearby window and daydreaming of happier memories associated with the room, she was jolted back to the present by a word she recognised. Todesstrafe. Death sentence. Again, the cold fear she had felt upon discovery of her betrayal gripped her. But her anger and outrage enabled her to keep her composure.

Pleading for mercy or begging for her life were not her style, especially in front of someone like the prosecuting lawyer who seemed to be waiting for just such a tearful outburst, assuming that a stylish, sophisticated, and willowy woman would lose most of her self-assurance upon hearing the death sentence pronounced. She thought of her father, whom she remembered as a strong and dashing figure in an officer's uniform. And Mona prided herself that whatever mettle had made her father the soldier he was, made Mona the woman she was. Later, she recalled the moment of her death sentence:

> I had steeled myself for this moment. I knew that all eyes were on me, expecting me to burst into tears. I was determined not to humble myself before any of them. As I left the courtroom, I put my heels together and bowed toward the judge, the prosecutor and my German counsel, who were standing together in a group. '*Guten morgen, meine herren* (Good morning, gentlemen),' I said.

If the prosecuting lawyer was infuriated with her self control, the judge was almost delighted. He followed her out of the court-room and quietly advised her that she could appeal the sentence. With calm self-assuredness, she informed him that this was exactly what she intended to do. There was no doubt that she had earned the respect of at least one person in that makeshift courtroom, and conceivably this was to play an important role in the events that followed.

Following the trial, Mona was transferred from Weteringschane to Amstelveense Prison, and a death cell. Upon arriving, however, she was given pen and paper to compose her appeal to General Franz Christiansen, "General der Flieger"—the highest ranking German officer in occupied Holland, and the man who had signed the death warrants for Brouwer, Besselink, Agterkamp, and van der Leek. Unfortunately, a copy of Mona's appeal has not survived, but in it she stated that he had friends in common with the Leonhardts, and she gave their names. Although uncertain this tactic would work, she tried it because she had nothing to lose. She wanted him to understand that if the world were still a sane place, they would be social peers capable of getting to know (and probably even like) each other. Mona sent off the appeal and waited, enduring gut-wrenching panic each time the cell door opened, wondering if her sentence was to be carried out as swiftly and unexpectedly as her trial had taken place.

According to Hans de Vries at RIOD, General Franz Christiansen did not have a reputation for overturning sentences. Something in Mona's letter affected him, or maybe the judge's admiration for Mona's calmness and self-control was evident in his assessment and struck a chord with Christiansen, because in mid-January Mona received word that her sentence had been commuted to life in prison. If she had mixed emotions about this decision, they were not immediately evident. She felt only relief that her life had been spared and wondered what they would do with her next.

She didn't have long to wait. In one of the few files salvaged after the Nazi surrender, there is a one-line entry dated January 17, 1942 stating that Mona Leonhardt was to serve a life sentence. Her destination is not listed. Such gaps in the documentation are a reminder that in the early days of the occupation, it wasn't just Dutch citizens who required time to organize themselves to resist fascist rule. The Nazis, too, needed time to organize systems and records, especially with the increasing number of people facing arrest for resistance activities. The only other date that appears in this brief record is that of Mona's trial. Shortly after that, she was summoned again from her cell to the prison office, to be told to prepare for transport via train to Germany. Her destination was the Anrath Penitentiary, near Krefeld in the Rheinland.

A compassionate clerk offered Mona a cup of hot tea while she awaited removal to the train. Mona was told to savour it, as it would be her last for a very long time. Left to contemplate the warning and her future, the door to the office opened and two or three male prisoners shuffled in, guarded by soldiers. Mona glanced at them, but didn't pay much attention at first. But one of the men looked familiar, and she allowed herself to scrutinize him. Joy mixed with horror as she realized that the man was her husband, Willem. He was thin and had dyed his hair and skin, but there was no doubt in her mind as to his identity. Her happiness at seeing him momentarily set aside the circumstances under which they were reunited. She dashed to embrace him, oblivious to the guards. They hugged long enough for her to utter in Dutch, "Have courage. Everything will be all right!" before the guards wrenched them apart. Once on the train to Germany, however, her happiness gave way to despair. Willem had been caught. By now she knew something of the treatment prisoners received at the hands of their Nazi captors, and she feared for Willem's life.

Given that most of the Leonhardts' acquaintances who had given substantial help to the airmen had been executed, and that others who had simply provided a rest-stop or a cup of tea were handed prison sentences, it is remarkable that Willem Leonhardt was still alive by mid-January. Willem's nephew, Gustav, recalled that Willem's father approached the Nazi authorities to try to arrange his son's release. He is reputed to have paid a large sum of money that, although it did not secure Willem's release, was sufficient to buy him a prison sentence, thereby sparing him a firing squad.

Few records remain from the Anrath Penitentiary. The facility was something of a clearing house for Dutch prisoners and it became especially crowded after the *Nacht und Nebel* decree. During the first year of the Nazi occupation, Dutch citizens suspected of anti-Nazi activity were housed in existing Dutch prisons. But after the decree was issued, more people were transported out of Holland to Germany, where escapes or attempts to break prisoners free would be more difficult. Because Krefeld was conveniently close to the Dutch-German border and because it had a large prison facility—Anrath—it became the first destination for many. When Anrath became too crowded, prisoners were moved to other prisons and camps within Germany.

Anrath Penitentiary was used prior to the war to house common criminals convicted of various offences, much as were Weteringschane and Amstelveense in Amsterdam. With the influx of foreign prisoners, no distinction was made between the criminals incarcerated at Anrath and those who, by today's standards, would be considered political prisoners. In many of the prisons and camps, prisoners' hair was shorn or shaved, either by each other or by guards. In many cases, all body hair, including pubic hair, was removed. While the reason for such action was ostensibly to prevent the spread of parasites, it had the additional effect of further depriving inmates of their individuality and self-esteem. Whether Mona was subjected to such treatment at Anrath is unknown, though she likely lost her hair, if not through shaving, then due to malnutrition. Victoria Tufts recalled that Mona also lost some, if not all of her teeth, partly because the tooth that had bothered prior to her arrest was not properly treated, resulting in the spreading of the infection and partly because nutrition in the prisons was so poor.

Upon arriving at Anrath, Mona was confined in a solitary cell with only a straw-filled mattress on which to sleep. Although the tiny room was cold, damp, and poorly lit, she did not mind being on her own. The smells that assaulted her nose—the sour-smelling straw mattress, the bucket that served as her toilet, her own unwashed body—were slightly more tolerable for having been mostly her own odours. But, after a couple of weeks, she was moved to another cramped cell with four straw mattresses on the floor, which she was forced to share with several other inmates. If life wasn't already bleak enough, exposure to common criminals and to mentally unstable prisoners, such as the young woman found guilty of murdering her illegitimate baby and shipping it to the father at the front, must have proved particularly disheartening. Others among Mona's cellmates included a woman from Luxembourg who had murdered her husband and then helped her lover murder his wife, and a German woman who had drowned her 17-year-old daughter. The only initial piece of good fortune was that the fleas and lice that nearly drove them mad in warmer weather were dormant.

If the prison at Anrath brought Mona in contact with vermin and society's most desperate, it also introduced her to those whose actions epitomized bravery and dignity in the face of inhumanity. Mona recalled after the war that a woman, whose husband had been the first French agent killed after the fall of France, had been forced to stand for the duration of her interrogation. A revolver at each cheek, she was ordered to give the names of others involved in the French resistance. She maintained her ignorance, and after 36 hours she was finally returned to her cell.

Another person who inspired Mona was a 60-year-old English woman named Mary Louise James. While working as the head of the YWCA in Paris, James had been arrested and sentenced to three years in prison for assisting a drunken American pilot whom she had found wandering the streets of occupied Paris. James had been starved with short rations, and she developed meningitis. Although gravely ill, she recovered, and with support from some influential people (among others, the Bishop of Rangoon and her brother-in-law, the Bishop of Gibraltar, and by the International Red Cross), she was allowed to return to England as part of a prisoner exchange. Before her departure, James had told Mona that the major contributing factor in her recovery was that she had been determined that no Nazi would ever prepare her body for burial nor bury her in Nazi soil. Those words stayed with Mona long after her own imprisonment ended

and helped give her courage to bear the harshness, the indigni-
ties, and the abuses as long as they lasted.

Prisoners were used as slave labour whenever possible, both
as a means of ensuring chores were done and as a way of further
demoralizing inmates. Following the war, through their studies
of the effects of prison conditions and treatment on prisoners of
war, psychologists determined that multiple degradations ren-
dered prisoners incapable of the desire to fight back or even to
feel strong emotions such as anger, compassion, and pain. It took
a Herculean effort to remain in touch with one's own humanity
and many people developed diverse means to maintain the last
shred, in the face of tasks that would otherwise have driven a
person mad. One of the tasks given to Mona was peeling sticky
paper off cardboard cartons that were to be reused. Mona
recalled finding crumbs in the bottom of biscuit boxes. Wetting
the tip of her finger with her tongue, she scraped out the last
remnants. If she came across a rare treasure—blobs of jam from
filled cookies on biscuit papers or boxes—she sucked the stains
until the hint of flavour was gone.

Another chore required of the inmates was knitting woollen
socks for German soldiers—a task frequently, though not solely,
assigned to prisoners who had been pulled from regular work
details due to illness. Mona was susceptible to respiratory ill-
nesses, and was likely a frequent visitor to the prison infirmary.
In fact, it's a wonder she didn't contract tuberculosis or pleurisy,
as did many other patients. And if she was ill frequently, it's
even more amazing that she was never selected for transport to
an extermination facility, as happened to so many *Nacht und
Nebel* prisoners who became sick.

Never very passive, Mona sabotaged, whenever possible, tasks
assigned to her. Every act of defiance, no matter how small, gave
her great satisfaction and contributed to her survival. When knitting socks for soldiers, prisoners were told that the end of wool
from one skein had to be spliced, not knotted to the next skein,
in order to avoid creating large knots in the socks that would
make walking uncomfortable for the Nazi soldiers who would
wear them. And there could be only three splices per sock.
Mona, who had proudly knitted socks for Canadian soldiers dur-

ing World War One, derived a great deal of satisfaction from deliberately breaking her wool frequently to make sure there would be large knots in the soles. Simply imagining the discomfort she was able to give numerous soldiers gave her immeasurable satisfaction and helped bolster her sagging spirits.

Forbidden to speak English, Mona would talk to herself, making up stories to occupy her mind and reciting poems she had memorized years before, knowing that speaking English meant a turn in solitary confinement or worse. On several occasions, Mona was caught or reported for speaking English, and suffered severe penalties. When she persisted in talking or singing to herself while in a solitary cell, she was subjected to abuse, both verbal and physical, by female *SS* guards.

From Anrath, Mona was sent to a prison in Wiedenbrück in September 1944—a small facility that housed more than two hundred female prisoners. Although records have been destroyed, rendering verification almost impossible, Mona remembered that near the prison at Wiedenbrück was a wood factory that had once belonged to a Jewish businessman. He and his family had been arrested and transported to the camps by the Nazis, who then took over the factory to manufacture plywood aircraft wings. Prisoners provided the labour, but their deteriorated physical condition meant that even a splinter could become life-threatening if infection set in.

During the war, German companies entered into agreements with prisons that would provide inmates as cheap labour, in exchange for money that was supposed to go to the prisoners' upkeep. Rarely were the funds used for the benefit of the prisoner—there was a ready supply of human slaves, and the Nazis needed the money elsewhere for their war effort. Despite the fact that factory work did not mean extra rations, it was still preferred over other labour, and was reserved for stronger, brighter prisoners, capable of working to meet a quota. Mona was assigned to a factory where she was detailed to splice wires in the manufacturing of bomb igniters. The task itself became mind-numbingly tedious, and knowing these efforts were helping to thwart or even kill Allied soldiers further eroded prisoner morale. After the war, in conversations with airman Richard

Pape, Mona would describe how she kept herself from breaking down mentally by varying the order of the coloured wires she had to assemble. And again, when possible, she sabotaged the work by not securing wires together firmly, hoping that her efforts meant that at least a few bombs would fail to detonate. After a very short time, the Nazis realized that political prisoners like Mona should not be used for this work because of the potential for sabotage. Foreign nationals were removed from factory detail and punished, then replaced by German prisoners serving time for criminal activity. With no igniters to build and little wood left for the manufacture of aircraft wings, there was little reason to keep political prisoners at Wiedenbrück any longer.

Right: Mona arrived at this Vechta train-station, transported by cattle car.

Vechta prison today. Here, Mona was last incarcerated, and escaped with Wendelien van Boetzelaer in the middle of an Allied bombing raid.

Chapter Ten

"dreaming of freedom"

In January 1945, Mona was crammed once more into the airless cattle car of a train, this time northbound for a prison in Vechta. The prison had been a reform school for girls prior to the war, but the inmates were released when the need for space to house foreign prisoners increased. Prisoners at Vechta represented almost every nationality at war with the Third Reich. One minor, but ultimately important difference between Vechta and the two other prisons where Mona had been an inmate, was the uniform. Unlike the dress at most prisons and camps (which ranged from civilian clothing removed from bodies of deceased prisoners to the pyjama-type uniform of the concentration camps), the prisoners' garb at Vechta was that used when it was a girls' reform school: dark blue denim skirt, white shirt, dark blue denim jacket, and dark hose.

Vechta was an important location to the German army for several reasons. First, there was an aerodrome at Vechta, a launching area for some of the night bombers that plagued England. Second, several railway routes converged in Vechta, linking the city with many other points in Germany. Third, there were a couple of hospitals in the vicinity, to which wounded German soldiers were brought by train for treatment. The function of both the male and female prisoners of war at Vechta was to provide support for these facilities, ensuring that the planes kept flying, trains kept moving, and patients at the hospitals were fed.

The kitchen at the Vechta Prison was one of the preparation sites for food distributed to the hospitals. Mona was assigned to peel mountains of potatoes, a major ingredient in the soups used to feed patients, who received full meals, and prisoners, who were given nothing besides the soup. By now, Mona was functioning almost entirely automatically. Although she received a few letters from Willem, by the time they arrived at the prison and were translated by Nazi authorities, there were considerable gaps in their content (letters written in English were translated into German before prisoners were permitted to read them, and passages were subject to censorship). Mona could never be certain whether Willem was still alive, until she received another letter. When she read a letter for the first time, she was assured of his existence, if only until she scanned the final lines. She knew she'd been in prison for a long time, since 1941, and the days blurred together. Hope of escape or rescue grew dimmer, though deep down she believed that freedom would come some day. Most of the time, it was difficult to remind herself of that. In the early days of the occupation when she and Willem were still living at Ingleside, she had written her family that "living isn't much worthwhile any more." How much bleaker it must have seemed to her by early 1945.

She had memorized some of the Psalms while a little girl at Sunday school, and was able to read them while a prisoner in Weteringschane because one of the books smuggled to her by a guard had been an English Bible. Undoubtedly, some of the passages and Psalms floated through her mind. She also distracted herself by recalling the plots of some of her favourite plays, which she repeated frequently to herself and occasionally to other inmates, in an effort to maintain her sanity.

In February 1945, yet another small group of prisoners was delivered to Vechta. One young woman was confined to her cell and not permitted to join the other prisoners for meals or exercise. Though initially unsure why her prison-mate had to abide by special restrictions, Mona felt sorry for her and attempted to make contact, if only to boost the young woman's spirits and to let her know she had one friend in the prison. At the end of her kitchen detail, Mona slipped a cooked potato undetected into a secret pocket that she had sewn in the skirt of her uniform for the purpose, and smuggled it to the young woman. Grateful, the newcomer accepted the gift.

The recent arrival introduced herself as Wendelien van Boetzelaer, a 22-year-old baroness and university student who had been rounded up with several others for prolonged resistance activity. This included having the means to employ a butler— except that her butler was actually an Allied airmen awaiting safe conduct out of the country. Newer to prison life than Mona, but with a similar dislike both for the occupation and the Nazis, the baroness had escaped twice and had been caught both times. This time the Nazis were intent on not allowing that to happen again.

Although Wendelien was struck by Mona's almost wild-eyed appearance and a cheerful demeanour that bordered on the manic, she recalled more than 50 years later that what impressed her most about Mona was her life force. With the inventive humour that seems to have been consistent among those who survived long terms in Nazi prisons and camps, Mona entertained her prison-mates with recipes. Mona was a gifted story-teller and she described lists of ingredients, detailed preparations, and the appearance of dishes in mouth-watering detail. At night, her deep, resonant voice, though speaking in hushed tones, carried in the darkness as she regaled her fellow inmates with instructions for dishes that, at times, seemed too fantastic to be real. Given Mona's sense of the dramatic, it's entirely possible that when she ran out of, or forgot recipes, she improvised new ones simply because she knew that her fellow prisoners had come to rely on her stories about food. When questioned about the apparent oddity and perhaps even cruelty of describing succulent dishes, rich desserts, and feasts to those who had not eaten properly in years, Wendelien laughs: "To those who have not food enough, such descriptions were almost enough to fill the stomach—and reminded us that we had something to look forward to when we regained our freedom. Simple pleasures were all we wanted. The Nazis might have deprived us of our freedom, but they couldn't take away our memories." Still, Wendelien also recalled stopping Mona once in mid-recipe, saying "But Mona! When shall we eat all this?"

Some of the recipes that Mona conveyed in limited correspondence to those outside the prison occasionally contained
unachievably huge proportions of ingredients, which has led
people to speculate that Mona was attempting to communicate
in code. While this certainly happened, as documented by
Germaine Tillion who was a prisoner at Ravensbrück and who
detailed some of the actions of her Nazi guards by disguising her
notes as recipes (described in her book *Ravensbrück*), it is doubtful that Mona's recipes were used for such a purpose. Reports
and anecdotes from prison camp survivors are almost universal
in their mention of the inflated role that food occupied in their
lives. Starvation-induced delirium may have inspired Mona's
fantastic recipes. The fact that Wendelien recalls Mona describing elaborate food preparations to amuse her fellow inmates at
night in the darkened cell would suggest that Mona's fascination
with food was borne of her love for cooking and an inadequate
diet. If the recipes had been a code, there would have been no
reason for Mona to share them with other inmates—especially if,
like Wendelien, they were unaware of a hidden meaning.

Mona quickly acquainted Wendelien with the hierarchy of the
prison. Because the facility had been a reform school prior to the
war, the head of the school, who was a civilian, had been
retained, along with most of the school's staff, who were also
civilians. Their numbers had been supplemented with members
of the *SS* to ensure proper watch was maintained over the steadi-
ly-increasing prison population in a facility already bursting at
the seams. The prison director, Mona had discovered, was not
like her Nazi counterparts. In fact, she was a lesbian, and as such
was not sympathetic to the Nazi persecution of homosexuals.
She had compassion for most of the women in her charge,
though she was not willing to risk her life or position for them.
As long as she was head of the prison, she could take care of the
women in some way. Imprisoned or dead, she could be of no
help. In fact, her replacement might well be a ruthless female *SS*
member. As Viktor Frankl, a psychotherapist and former prisoner
of Auschwitz wrote in *Man's Search for Meaning*: "It was apparent that the mere knowledge that a man was either a camp guard
or a prisoner tells us almost nothing. Human kindness can be

found in all groups, even those which as a whole would be easy to condemn."

As it was, the prison director at Vechta tried to make her charges' lives as bearable as possible, which was difficult in a damp and poorly-heated building and with the *SS* looking on. Each inmate was issued a small piece of clay soap and, once a week, was given a small bowl of cold water in which she was expected to wash herself and her clothes. On occasion Mona was jeered at by prisoners and guards alike for her attempts at personal grooming—small but important vestiges of her humanity and her sense of self. Cramped, stark cells had to accommodate more people than they were designed to hold, and prisoners slept on wooden bunks. The bucket which served as a toilet stood in the middle of the room and afforded no privacy. It was removed once a day to be emptied, and creosote was splashed in the bottom as a disinfectant. The smell of unwashed bodies and clothing, overlaid with the odour of creosote, was nauseating. There was little the director could do to alleviate these conditions, which were prescribed by Nazi regulations.

At each of the prisons, Mona had seen that even those of a privileged and refined background could behave as little more than animals. She saw women fight over food rations, threaten each other for preferred sleeping spaces, and report fellow inmates for the most minor misdemeanours in an effort to curry favour with the guards. Even Mona was reduced to scurrying "like a rat" to grab a small piece of apple that had fallen to the floor from a guard's mouth before anyone could deprive her of it. Depressed and dismayed at the erosion of their dignity and humanity, Mona helped organize a system that would help her and fellow inmates retain some degree of civility. They agreed that when rations were delivered, portions would be divided so that the oldest prisoner would receive the largest rations, with the youngest to receive the smallest. Exceptions were made if one of the prisoners was ill. Mona, who had frequently suffered from sinusitis, bronchitis, and other respiratory ailments before having to endure prison life, was one of those who fell sick. Medicine was in short supply—almost unheard of—and the only recourse for the prison doctor was to order extra rations, partly because Mona was ill and partly because she was affiliated with a "good, Dutch family." Though sick, Mona resented the class distinction, and shared her extra rations with her cellmates.

Mona persuaded the prison director to let Wendelien out of her cell to join the rest of the prisoners for work tasks, meals, and for exercise. Although daily life in the prison was bleak, Mona knew it was better to be with the general population than cooped up alone in a damp cell every cold winter day. When assigned to kitchen duties, both women smuggled pieces of cooked potatoes to share with women assigned to other tasks in the prison. And if cooked potatoes weren't available, they settled for raw. Regular prison meals consisted of a thin, watery, cabbage-based broth in which were, when available, pieces of carrot, turnip, or other fodder generally used to feed livestock. For a long time after the war ended, the smell of cooking cabbage made Wendelien gag. Although meat was desirable, prisoners were often suspicious if they found some in the stock, not knowing its source. Usually it had come from horses, cattle, or other livestock killed by bombs or artillery. On one occasion, Wendelien found an eye floating in the cloudy liquid that had been slopped in her bowl. She determined by its size that it had belonged to a cow, but could not bring herself to eat the soup even after she had discarded the eye.

Exercise in the prison yard consisted of prisoners shuffling along single file in a circle. Talk was most dangerous during these sessions because every guard posted at strategic locations about the yard was a member of the SS. They were swift to silence a prisoner attempting to talk to another prisoner, and were more vicious in their punishment than the non-SS guards. The exercise was torturous for malnourished women dressed in thin clothing. The pace at which they needed to walk to create some warmth was not allowed, and so they struggled along, enduring the cold until they could seek shelter inside the old building, which wasn't much warmer but which at least offered some protection from the elements.

On returning indoors after one such session, Wendelien quickly told Mona that she was going to attempt another escape. As soon as she had the opportunity, Mona asked Wendelien how and when she would accomplish this. Wendelien said she didn't know; an opportunity was sure to present itself, in time, and both of them had to be ready to seize it. Although Mona had dreamed of freedom, escape had never seemed a possibility. Caught between thrill and dread, she didn't have to wait long before a chance to escape arose.

Just after the middle of March, Mona and Wendelien noticed an increase in plane traffic in the skies over Vechta. Although the Nazis responded with anti-aircraft fire, retaliation from Allied planes was limited, except for the destruction of railway lines in the area. Mona and Wendelien expected an air attack was imminent, and surmised that the planes overhead were on missions beyond bombing selected targets. Daily life continued to be fairly, though uneasily, quiet. The women did not know that the Allies, under the command of Field Marshall Bernard Montgomery and Major-General George Patton, were positioning themselves for a push across the Rhein in two strategic locations: at Oppenheim and near Düsseldorf. But their instincts told them preparations for something much bigger were underway by the Allies. In anticipation of her next opportunity to escape, Wendelien asked the prison director for a sweater that was among the belongings taken from her when she was admitted to the prison. She cited the bone-chilling dampness and her rheumatism as grounds for needing extra warmth, but her real reason was to have an extra piece of non-prison-issue clothing on her when the time came to escape. Buoyed by her success, Wendelien encouraged Mona to ask for her shoes on the same grounds—that the wooden prison clogs were inadequate to keep her feet warm. If the prison director suspected the real reason for their requests, she never let on.

Mona's escape to freedom: 22-year-old Wendelien van Boetzelaer and Mona Parsons fled Vechta prison and walked as far as the border town of Rhede before being separated. Their entire route from Nazi Germany to occupied Holland was stricken with Allied bombs, desperate Nazis, and half-starved people. Mona made it as far as the Dutch town of Vlagtwedde, where the Allies transported her to Canadian Rear Headquarters in Oldenburg, Germany—only a few miles from where she began her trek.

Chapter Eleven

"a daring escape"

anadian War Diary accounts of the final days of March 1945 describe air sorties on various targets in Germany within a hundred miles of the Dutch border near Krefeld, in an effort to disrupt Nazi transportation and communication lines. When aircraft were grounded by bad weather, ground troops kept up the barrage and prevented Nazi forces from making any gains. Two particular entries in the Daily Ops (Operations) Summaries of 12 Canadian Army Air Liaison Section, 143 Wing, show the tide of the war beginning to change significantly. March 22: "Later in the day the war's critical phase was confirmed by the arrival of Mr. Winston Churchill on the aerodrome." March 23: "The lull before the storm gave us 15 rails cuts in the morning."

The Daily Ops Summary for March 24 continues as follows: "Everything obviously centred around this superb operation—crossing the Rhine—the pilots were briefed in detail by G/C Nesbitt and W/C Grant at 9 P.M. the previous night, then again at 0500 hours for their particular objectives....Armed with 500 pound clusters, the 2 squadrons kept 4 a/c in the area from 0930-1330, bombing out any gun positions requested, then each section stooged around at from one to three thousand feet spraying every gun flash that was observed..." Some of the gun positions mentioned were at Vechta. And Mona and Wendelien found themselves in the midst of this barrage that was, at once, terrifying in its fury and exhilarating in its potential for escape.

On March 22, 1945, Patton's troops crossed the Rhein at Oppenheim; at the same time, about 150 miles down river from Patton's location, Montgomery was completing preparations for his troops' surge across the Rhein at Wesel. Late at night on March 23, Operation Plunder was launched with a tremendous bombardment. Early the next morning, March 24, Operation Varsity augmented Plunder, while members of the North Nova Scotia Highlanders were part of the force that readied itself to continue the advance, observed from an Allied command post by Winston Churchill. One wonders what Mona's reaction would have been had she known that her fellow Nova Scotians were so near at hand and about to play a supporting role in her dramatic bid for freedom. Records in the War Diary only hinted at the magnitude of the battle, recording events as they unfolded, but those who beheld this invasion—including members of the North Nova Scotia Highlanders—were indelibly impressed. As one Highlander later recounted:

It was during this waiting that the Novas beheld the airborne assault, a sight to stay with them in memory. The sky to the northwest was almost black with the approaching aircraft carrying airborne troops. Thousands of gliders and carriers filled the heavens like a great swarm of bees. The sight was amazing, overpowering, making indelible imprints on the minds of those who witnessed it. With the air almost filled with the thunder of Allied guns and the sky teeming with aircraft, the whole military might of the Allied forces seemed to be concentrated on the area just ahead, and such a display of force could not but hearten the attackers and dismay the defenders.

The inmates were just starting their workday when the Allied attack was unleashed on their position. They hardly had a chance to notice the drone of planes overhead before the bombs began falling and exploding around them. Presumably, the Allied targets were the aerodrome and the railway, but the prisons for both men and women were near these targets and dropping bombs from planes is hardly a precision manoeuvre during a full-scale air strike. The women watched in helpless horror as the men's prison took a direct hit and exploded in flames.

Guards and inmates at Vechta were frozen with momentary confusion before recovering sufficiently to head toward shelters in the basement of the prison. The director, concerned about the fate of her charges, unlocked the prison gates and shouted that the prisoners had a choice. They could go to the prison's bomb shelter, as she assumed the male prisoners had done—and they all had seen what happened there—or they could take their chances outside in the hail of bombs and gunfire. Like so many others throughout the Nazi regime, the director, who was not a member of the *SS*, was well aware that the war was reaching its conclusion. She didn't know what would happen to her prisoners, or what orders might be issued concerning their collective fate if her superiors panicked in the face of the rapidly advancing Allies. The director had no chance to reconsider her offer before Wendelien grabbed Mona's hand, and both women bolted out into the mayhem.

At regular intervals around the airfield, German soldiers had dug pillboxes—foxholes lined with concrete—large enough to accommodate two people, in preparation for possible attack. Although heavy smoke partially obscured their surroundings, Wendelien relied on instinct and the grace of God to take them toward the airfield and the temporary shelter of the pillboxes. They were rewarded within minutes as they dropped into one. They paused just long enough to catch their breath and to sight the next hole in line, before clambering out and desperately racing toward the next.

"I don't know what we used for energy," mused the baroness 53 years later. "Especially Mona. She was particularly thin and weak. She had been in Nazi prisons for more than three years. But then, maybe that's what drove her on."

They had made their way along about half the airfield when they suddenly encountered a young German soldier in one of the pillboxes they tumbled into. Wendelien recalled that it was difficult to tell who was more surprised—him or them. He tried to sound authoritative as he ordered them back to the prison. Wendelien assured him that they had been on a work detail outside the prison when the air raid had started, and that they would return just as soon as the bombing stopped. And with that, she scrambled out of the hole, dragging Mona after her. They dashed to the next hole, hoping that the smoke would provide some cover before the soldier had a chance to pursue them or grab his gun.

At last they reached the end of the airfield and sought cover in nearby trees. With the attack still raging around them, they headed toward the town centre in the hope of finding shelter. Each home or shop they approached was deserted and their shouts went unheard or unheeded. They took to the road again, heading toward a forest at the edge of the town where they hoped they could rest and wait out the air raid. Not far into the woods, however, they came across a large munitions dump guarded by a single soldier. They weren't as worried about being detected by him as they were about the devastation that would occur if a single Allied bomb or shell found its way to that site.

Fear prevailed over exhaustion, and the two proceeded in what they thought was a westerly direction toward Holland; without a map or a compass, they couldn't be entirely certain of their course. The women halted briefly to remove the prison aprons they'd been wearing, which they buried in mud on the roadside, and for Wendelien to take the sweater she had been wearing under her uniform and put it over top. The denim clothing issued by the prison was common work garb worn by farmers. Attired this way, the women would easily blend into the communities where they would seek food and shelter. Gradually, the relentless bombing subsided, and as night approached they found shelter in the barn of a deserted farm. There, for the first time in their brief reacquaintance with liberty, they began to realize that they were, indeed, free. There was little time to examine their rapidly changing emotions—disbelief, exhilaration, fear, giddiness, panic, the desire to laugh, shriek, and cry all at once— because most pressing was the need to decide their next step. The quiet and safety of the barn provided them with their first opportunity to assess their situation and discuss their strategy for returning home.

Wendelien was fluent in several languages, including a few German dialects. Extensive travel in the country had given her a solid grasp of German geography—a good thing, since they were faced with covering about a hundred kilometres in order to reach the Dutch border, and only then if they were able to travel in a straight line. Wendelien, who had escaped twice during her 18-month incarceration, was more keenly aware than Mona of what might lie ahead. Twice when her identity had been discovered, she had been turned over to Nazi authorities by German citizens who were loyal to the Führer. This time, her escape was complicated by the presence of another person, one who could not be passed off as German. Mona could understand and speak German, but she spoke it with a distinct accent that would immediately give away their ruse. Mona suggested that, under the circumstances, her greatest asset was her actor training. Indeed, the only way to carry off such a daring escape was for Mona to pose as a mentally-challenged women with a speech impediment, and for Wendelien to play her niece.

Their chosen disguise was not without risk. In October 1939, Hitler had implemented Aktion T 4—a program of systematic euthanasia to rid the country of the infirm, deformed, disabled, and chronically ill. Though the program was initially aimed at infants and children, it was quickly applied to the rest of the population, young and old, and then to ethnic groups like Jews and Gypsies. Killings were carried out in six centres around Germany until August 1941, when a Catholic bishop, Clemens von Galen, decried the program as "plain murder" from the pulpit of Münster Cathedral. The Nazis retaliated by arresting and beheading three of von Galen's parish priests, (though they would not risk punishing von Galen for fear he would become a martyr). Although the Nazis officially suspended Aktion T 4, their policy of exterminating the infirm—which included "senile disorders, retardation, and other neurological conditions"—continued on an unofficial basis, as did their large-scale killing of Jews and Gypsies.

Despite these risks, Mona and Wendelien knew that this plan was their only hope to make it across Germany. Beginning to feel the exhilaration of freedom, Mona revelled in rehearsing, though Wendelien, extremely cautious and vigilant after her re-arrests, had serious concerns about their ability to succeed—but this wasn't sufficient reason to give up. The next morning, they

found a coffee shop, which appeared to be deserted. While looking around for its owners, they noticed a map of the region on
the wall of the shop. Wendelien was able to discern that they
were heading in a westerly direction. Because she had followed
this route in a previous escape attempt, with disastrous results,
she decided that they should head northwest for a while, then
west to find a point at which to cross the Dutch border.
Wendelien and Mona set out in the direction of Cloppenburg,
about 25 kilometres away.

While their greatest concern was evading recapture, the two
women also had to contend with inclement weather and continuing Allied assaults from the air and on the ground. For the first
few days they enjoyed fairly warm temperatures and sunshine,
but soon temperatures dipped near the freezing point. And if
these conditions weren't miserable enough, the women's discomfort was exacerbated by rain and drizzle. War diaries for the period shortly after the push across the Rhein record that Allied
planes continued to target rail lines and were also directed by
ground forces to destroy roads and other potential escape routes,
and to flush enemy troops out of areas like forests, which afforded cover against the advancing Allies. Most haunting are the
notes that recorded planes having strafed civilian convoys.
Sometimes it was possible to identify these as such before bombs
were released, but this was not always the case, and occasionally
bombs were dropped on civilian targets before Allied pilots were
able to identify them.

Nazi plans to sabotage the Allied advance were a huge concern at this point in the fighting. There were reports of pro-Nazi
French and Dutch soldiers posing as Allied reinforcements separated from their units, but in fact planted by the Nazis to sabotage the Allied advance. In other incidents reported by German
prisoners of war, members of a Nazi underground movement
were instructed to mingle with civilians to disrupt, resist, and
sabotage the Allies. US Army Intelligence passed on information
gleaned from *Wehrwolf*, a pamphlet that instructed women in the
German underground to blend with the civilian population. On
receiving a second code word—*Wehrwolf*—they were to begin
subversive activities in individual squads. "Turn day into night,

night into day!" the pamphlet incited its supporters. "Hit the enemy wherever you meet him. Be sly! Steal weapons, ammunition, and rations! Women, support the battle of the *Wehrwolf* wherever you can!"

Because of their prison-induced isolation, Mona and Wendelien had no way of knowing about *Wehrwolf* or any other resistance activities organized by the Nazis against the Allies. Nor could they guess that Allied soldiers had been put on their guard about women they might encounter in war zones. But it would prove to be another factor in the risky escape the two were undertaking.

Shortly after embarking on their escape route, Wendelien and Mona had a chance to test their aunt-and-niece routine on a local farmer whom they stopped to ask for food. Neither the farmer nor his wife suspected anything, instead offering the two "refugees" an egg, white bread, and coffee—and Mona thought it an entirely appropriate way to mark her father's birthday which coincided with the day, March 25. They fared equally well at their next stop, although the food they were given there had consequences for Mona. Offered a bowl of thick pea soup that contained more fat than Mona and Wendelien were accustomed to, Mona was plagued with severe stomach cramps and became ill. Once again they were given shelter at a farmhouse, where they were offered the unbelievable luxury of a feather bed. Because the women's feet were in such horrible shape, the farmer let them stay an extra day. They marvelled at their good fortune as they were treated to delicious farm fare—including pastries. They did chores for the farmer, whose wife provided Mona and Wendelien with clean bandages for their blistered feet before they continued their journey. Chores were the currency with which they paid for food and shelter at various farms for the next few days, working their way westward to Sögel, about 40 kilometres from Cloppenburg, 65 kilometres from where they had started. Elated but cautious in their newly-gained freedom, the women enjoyed the fairly warm, mild weather for the first few days of their trek to Holland. But they found it discouraging when it began to rain and the weather became cold and raw. To complicate matters, the farther north and west they pushed, the boggier the ground became, and the greater their struggle to cover as much distance as possible. Neither woman's footwear was equal to the task and, after plaguing them with blisters, the shoes gave out altogether, forcing them to proceed barefoot in the chilling temperatures.

Near Sögel, they hitched a ride with a farmer hauling beer kegs in his horse-drawn cart and were amazed when the fellow, who had struck them as even-tempered and jovial, began railing about the Nazis. They had not heard such sentiments expressed by any of the German citizens they had encountered so far, though most were sick of the war and wished it would end. This farmer, however, wasn't holding back; he resented what had been done to the country, he told them, and was convinced that once Germans got rid of "the Nazi mob," the country would once again prosper. They fell silent for a while as the horse slowly drew the cart down the road, until they noticed a large group of people being herded along by soldiers. Later, Mona described to a Canadian war correspondent her horror. "The sight of them went through me like an electric shock. It haunted me for days, and it still haunts me. I had never seen anything like it in all my years in prison. They all looked so young and yet so old. Some of them faltered, and, when their companions couldn't hold them up, the Hitler Jugend guards would beat them with long whips." The farmer looked sorrowfully at the starving men, who were being marched from a work-to-death camp in the Meppen area in advance of Canadian troops. He looked at their brutal treatment at the hands of mere boys, then growled that this was one of the reasons Germany would be better off without the Nazis. Sharing the farmer's bounty that night, Mona found it difficult to enjoy her food, knowing that most of the men she'd seen earlier that day probably would not survive much longer. And then she thought it might be a blessing if they did not.

Around Sögel, they began to encounter much heavier fighting, and were forced to turn north again. The route prolonged their stay in Germany, but they consoled themselves that each painful step took them farther away from prison and closer to home. One evening toward nightfall they found themselves in a small village, where they received a terrifying reminder that, no matter how much distance they put between themselves and prison, they were still in dangerous territory. They stopped a man on the street to ask where they could find shelter, too late realizing that he was a wearing a Nazi armband—a local police officer. He told them that he was sheltering several refugees in his home and invited them to stay there. To decline would have invited suspicion, so they had no choice but to accept.

Mona acted her most deranged, mostly because she was terrified their secret would be discovered. But her feigned dementia also put them at great risk. Wendelien, too, was concerned, though she had no choice but to remain calm. They were introduced to others who were staying at the house, and at one point, one of the refugees overheard Mona whisper something to Wendelien. Alarmed, he accused Mona of not speaking proper German. Both women were momentarily terrified, but Wendelien's calm and quick thinking helped convince everyone that he had misheard Mona, who really could not speak intelligibly at all. Realising the danger they were in, Wendelien suggested that Mona remain in their loft sleeping quarters in the barn rather than join everyone at the evening meal, and Wendelien would say that the large group of people in the house had had a bad effect on Mona's nerves. Hoping to elicit their sympathy and downplay Mona's apparent mental weakness, Wendelien explained that her aunt had been fine until she had learned that her husband had been killed in the war. Although Mona had to forego the evening meal, it was a small price to pay. Even after everyone had retired for the night, Mona and Wendelien continued to play their roles, for fear that someone might overhear them if they attempted to talk to each other. Both women were greatly relieved to leave the next morning and resume their journey toward Holland.

After three weeks of walking and working their way across Germany, the women reached the Ems River at the Küsten Canal near Dorpen. They chose to cross the Ems at this point, because they could detect no signs of German soldiers—that is, until they were halfway across the bridge. By then it was too late to turn back. The soldiers had seen them. They continued across the bridge and were stopped at the checkpoint. Challenged for their papers, Wendelien calmly replied that they were Dutch refugees who had been driven out of Arnhem by the fighting, adding that they had been so thankful to get out with their lives, they had given little thought to their papers. When asked where they had fled after Arnhem, Mona felt a flicker of panic. But Wendelien didn't hesitate. She replied that they had gone to Mönchengladbach. Mona's panic gave way to confusion. They hadn't discussed any of this. Wendelien was obviously improvising like mad, and Mona silently prayed that the guard would be convinced. Mona's heart skipped several more beats when the soldier asked where they had stayed in Mönchengladbach. Once again Wendelien did not falter, but gave an address. Mona nearly fainted with relief when the soldier remarked that he lived in Mönchengladbach and knew the address. Later, when Mona asked Wendelien how she had thought it all up, Wendelien calmly replied that she would never risk giving a false address, and had used one belonging to friends of her parents, whom she had visited in Mönchengladbach in 1937. Mona was nearly delirious with relief and joy.

Fighting in the area was extremely heavy and they found themselves pushed a little farther north, where they wandered into Rhede, a small town on the German side of the Dutch border. There, they found a priest whom they asked for help. He introduced them to the burgomeister, who also asked them for their papers. Any apprehension the two women felt at confessing they had no papers turned to relief when he offered to provide them with new ones. After swearing an affidavit, Mona and Wendelien were given identity papers and a place where they could stay for the night while other accommodations were found. The burgomeister quietly suggested that Wendelien might want to leave her aunt behind to be cared for by others, but she firmly declined. Later, Wendelien and Mona were told that the burgomeister was sheltering about 30 refugees in his own house, half of whom were deserters from the German army.

Whatever relief Mona and Wendelien might have felt at being so close to Holland turned to despair the next day when they were told the only accommodations available were on two separate farms. Once again, they would have to work for their keep, tending animals, doing farm chores, or helping with household tasks. Mona would have to continue her ruse alone, and Wendelien would visit as often as she could.

Wendelien's hosts were fairly prosperous farmers with three children. Mona did not fare as well. She was placed with a poor family, the head of which was a milchräder—a person who had no dairy herd of his own, but who collected milk from local farmers and delivered it to customers. There were six children in the family, most of whom took delight in goading Mona, whom they had been told was mentally challenged. They taunted her, pushed her around, lifted her skirt and, assuming her to be deaf as well, shouted at her. Food was scarce, and the farm was run-down and dirty. Mona shared a bed with the eldest child, a girl of about 13, who had open sores on her legs and feet—presumably from a combination of flea bites, malnutrition and unsanitary conditions. Mona, too, had weeping sores on her feet from flea bites and from blisters which had become infected during her long trek through Germany. She was petrified she would contract something from sharing a bed with the girl, but there was little she could do. After noticing that the pail into which the cow was milked was also used for carrying water from a nearby open ditch, and for rinsing out the baby's diapers, Mona avoided drinking anything but black coffee.

Wendelien visited Mona frequently, preferring to meet her in one of the fields so that they could speak to one another in English. Even this caused Wendelien some concern because Mona's deep voice carried, even when speaking in a whisper. Wendelien laughed about it more than 50 years later, but can still recall her alarm that, after being told to keep her voice down, the best Mona could manage was a stage whisper. Wendelien was convinced that anyone standing at the edge of the field would be able to hear her every word. But she also recalls that, although Mona was a superb actor, she must have found it very trying to keep up the disguise she had chosen, partly because she could never let her guard down and partly because it required a great deal of concentration. Especially nerve-wracking for Mona was her concern that she might talk in her sleep.

During one of their field visits, Mona and Wendelien discussed the next step in their plan to get home. Both women
knew that Holland was almost as close as the end of a field, but
they also knew they would be foolhardy to try to simply walk
away one day, or attempt to flee under cover of night. Wendelien
had repeatedly cautioned against acting precipitously—sage
advice from a woman who had been recaptured twice and now
found herself close enough to Dutch soil to see it. Fighting had
become very heavy in the area surrounding them, and Wendelien
felt it best to avoid inviting suspicion and to hold their position
in Rhede, where they had both food and shelter. Besides, all
around was boggy marshland—in fact, most of the territory was
dykeland that stretched from Holland to Germany—and they
knew that if they wandered off the path inadvertently, they
would put themselves in greater peril than their disguises as
refugees. However, when days dragged on with little hope for
change, they finally agreed that if weather conditions were
right—such as a fairly clear, moonlit night during a lull in fighting—they would risk making their way across the fields and over
the bog to Holland.

Canadian troops in Holland, spring 1945.

Chapter Twelve

"honey, hot tea, and chocolate"

So rapid was the Allied advance into the area around Rhede that a notation in the War Diaries indicated that the military were scrambling to produce maps of the battle zones because they changed so frequently. Consequently, Mona and Wendelien's planned escape to Holland was altered by the Allies' ever-changing battle plans. The Canadian infantry had been busy liberating northeastern Holland in late March and early April, and the Canadian Armoured Division re-entered Germany to take Meppen on April 8. From there, the Armoured Division set a course for Oldenburg. In the meantime, fighting became particularly vicious after the Polish Armoured Division crossed the Küsten Canal in an area only a few kilometres from Rhede.

Suddenly, the fighting that had been taking place around Rhede now moved closer. The bump of artillery, which had been daily background sounds for Mona and Wendelien, became the buzz and roar of shells exploding in their midst. The Polish offensive and Canadian efforts sent the Nazis into a rear guard action. Artillery shells began bursting in the fields as farmers, their families, and labourers scrambled for cover. The milchräder's wife grabbed some food and bedding and herded her children into the basement. Mona favoured taking her chances above ground to being in the close confines of a cramped, dusty cellar, which reminded her too much of prison. She remained on the main floor of the house until the farmer emerged to check on the battle's progress during a brief lull. He went outside to speak to a German soldier and to offer him food. In a flash, an artillery shell landed nearby, exploding on impact and sending a plume of earth skyward. Mona flung herself on the floor before she could see what happened to the farmer and the soldier, then decided that the cellar was preferable to the ground floor of the house if the next shell landed on the building. Joining the rest of the family in the cellar, Mona huddled in a corner on a mat while the battle raged over their heads.

When at last the assault stopped three days later, Mona and the farmer's eldest daughter ventured out to find the farmer. The first sight that greeted them was the farmer's feet sticking up from the ditch. Nearby was the soldier, with the sausage the farmer had given him still clutched in one hand. The child began to wail and ran back to the house to get her mother. Mona and the farmer's widow struggled to carry the body into the house. They had only just laid the corpse on a sofa in the parlour when neighbours burst into the house to warn them that the Polish army was advancing on the town. Mona wondered desperately what had happened to Wendelien. She couldn't think of a way she could try to reach her, without giving away her disguise. Remembering the escape route she had discussed with Wendelien, she decided to take it, hoping that Wendelien had done the same thing. Following their planned route across the bog with the farmer's wife and family, she saw no sign of Wendelien among the many others who were heading in the same direction. The going was difficult as the two women and the eldest girl pushed and pulled, through icy muck and puddles, a small wagon filled with younger children and a few hastily-grabbed household items. While aeroplanes strafed nearby targets, artillery shells continued to fall, punctuated by distant bursts of machine-gun fire. Not knowing whether they were heading into a zone of heavy fighting or away from it, they pressed on. Mona hoped she would encounter Wendelien at one of the farmhouses where some Rhede residents sought shelter, but was disappointed to find not a trace.

It would be several months before Mona learned Wendelien's fate. When shelling started, Wendelien was a couple of kilometres away from her billet, helping her host-farmer milk his cows. Leaving behind everything but the milk they had gathered, they headed back to the farm. A shell landed close to them, but did not detonate. They made it back to the farmhouse to load the farmer's wife, parents, and children on a cart with some bedding and food as quickly as possible. Most Germans feared capture by the enemy, and their terror was understandable when it came to the Poles, who had a deep hatred of Nazi Germany. As the Polish infantry advanced, its soldiers set fire to most of the farmhouses in the area. When the shelling ended, a single farmhouse remained standing only because a Russian prisoner of war, who had been assigned as slave labour to the farmer, attested that he had been well-treated, allowed to eat with the family, and given a comfortable bed.

The family with whom Wendelien had been billeted joined with several others in their flight before the advancing Polish infantry. Their route of escape—the main road leading to the Allies' next major target, Leer—was also the target of artillery bombardment. The group fled to a field where they knew they would find an earthen hut. They found temporary shelter there, taking turns digging a large trench in which all 40 or 50 people could take cover. To complicate matters further, they had picked up several wounded German soldiers among the dead along the side of the road. The Poles must have seen some Nazi uniforms among the group's number, because each time someone put their head out, it was greeted with a burst of machine-gun fire. For two or three days, the cluster of Germans remained in their temporary shelter until, at last, the women in the group decided to take action, knowing that food supplies were running out, and that the wounded needed medical attention.

Using their bed linen to make large white flags, the women loaded their children into the prams and carts they had brought with them. Holding the flags and clasping hands, the women cautiously stepped from their hiding place and walked toward the road, hoping the Poles would not shoot at a vulnerable and defenceless group. The soldiers held their fire and allowed the women and children to approach. Once the situation was explained, the group was permitted to move into the shelter of the last remaining farmhouse. After another day watching the wounded deteriorate, Wendelien took a bicycle she had found and placed behind her on the seat a young German soldier who had suffered a head wound. Supporting his weight on her back, she cycled down the road to a first aid station staffed by Polish medics. To the amazement of the personnel there, she explained that she was Dutch and an escaped prisoner of war, seeking medical attention for a Nazi soldier. They told her she should let him die. Her response was simple. "If I am able to forgive him, you should be able to treat him." They began to tend to the young soldier, and Wendelien continued her trek to Holland by bicycle.

Farther along the road, Wendelien encountered a first aid station staffed by Canadians. By that time, she was exhausted and in need of food and medical attention. Soldiers at the station gave her a cup of coffee and showed her a copy of Life magazine, which featured photos of Bergen-Belsen. She was stunned to learn that the horrors she and Mona had seen near Meppen had not been isolated. Wendelien was told that an ambulance would take her to a Canadian hospital where she could receive better attention for the septicaemia evident from the tell-tale red lines that were slowly creeping up her legs. Another shock awaited her in the ambulance, when she realized that she would have to share it with a French-Canadian soldier who had been wounded in both legs, and who was apparently delirious—brandishing a dagger and shouting that he wanted to get back to the fighting.

At the Canadian hospital, Wendelien was given a bed among the wounded and the dying. Shortly after her arrival, a Canadian soldier in the next bed died of his wounds. Knowing she was hungry, and probably loath to waste the food, the nurse offered Wendelien the soldier's rations. Despite her hunger, Wendelien found she had no appetite.

In the meantime, Mona and the farmer's family pushed on until they'd put about ten kilometres between themselves and Rhede. The ravaged countryside had little impact on Mona, who was intent on determining whether they were definitely in Dutch territory, and on finding shelter. Spying a farmhouse, the women stopped to ask for assistance. Mona's heart leapt with joy when the woman who answered the door of the farmhouse spoke to them in Dutch. She was back in Holland! Hope and optimism soared, despite her weakened physical condition and the sores on her feet which now showed definite signs of infection. Confident that she ran no risk of recapture, Mona decided to drop her disguise as a cleft-palated, mentally-challenged woman and reveal her identity to both the German farmer's wife and to the owners of the Dutch farm where they now sought shelter. While the German woman stood agape upon learning that Mona's disabilities had been carefully contrived, the Dutch couple were delighted to learn that not only was Mona Canadian, but was married to a Dutch citizen. The Dutch woman embraced Mona and asked if she had any idea of the role undertaken by her Canadian compatriots in the battle to wrest Holland from Nazi control. Mona confessed she knew nothing, and the Dutch woman recounted the activities of Canadian liberators in easing the hunger and the general suffering of the Dutch population since arriving in the Netherlands. Although the Dutch farmers urged Mona to remain longer than overnight, they understood her desire to return to Laren and knew that she still had a significant distance to cover—about 200 kilometres. Mona's hosts gave her a parcel of food, some clothing, fresh bandages for her feet, and a pair of wooden clogs before she set out again to walk back to Laren. Sheer determination and the generosity of people along the way had brought Mona this far, and she was convinced that these, combined with the exhilaration of being back in Holland, were all that she needed to help her complete the final leg of her odyssey.

Despite what she had seen and endured in Germany, Mona was unprepared for the devastation of the Dutch countryside. The country was just emerging from the Hongerwinter of 1944-45, precipitated when the Nazis cut off food supplies to the Dutch nation as punishment for its dogged resistance to Nazi occupation. And the battles between advancing Allies and retreating Nazis had laid waste to the countryside. Rotting carcasses of livestock dotted the fields, hulks of military vehicles were strewn along muddy roadsides. In some places, corpses of soldiers and civilians lay amid the rubble and ruins of what once were homes, farms, and villages. Those left alive were as thin and ragged as Mona herself. For the first time, Mona felt defeated and wondered if there was any point in returning home. Would her house even be standing? What had been Willem's fate? How many of her friends would still be in Laren? She stopped to rest near Vlagtwedde, at a farmhouse in the midst of what had obviously been a battle zone, just a few kilometres from the Dutch farmhouse where she had heard stories of heroic Canadians fighting to liberate the country and bring food to a starving nation. Minutes after she sat down to ponder her next step, an old man pedalled up to the house on a bicycle. Mona told him how she had come to be there and where she wanted to go. The fellow told her that he had passed British troops not much further down the road and he offered to take her to them. She gladly accepted a lift on the back of his bicycle.

The first soldier Mona saw was loading a truck. Although she had never seen Canadian battledress, she approached him hopefully, and with as much confidence as she could muster. For a wealthy woman used to dressing in the height of fashion, she now weighed only 87 pounds, was filthy and clad in shabby clothes, wearing wooden clogs over her bandaged feet. The soldier responded gruffly when Mona approached him and asked if he spoke English. He was intent on maintaining his guard in the event she was involved with *Wehrwolf*. But his abruptness quickly changed to amazement at hearing that she had escaped from a Nazi prison and then walked across Germany. His amazement doubled when she identified herself as Canadian. Trying to maintain the distance he'd been ordered to keep when dealing with a possible *Wehrwolf* member, he asked with suspicion where she was from. When she replied that her home was in a little town in Nova Scotia called Wolfville, he nearly dropped the box he was holding. He told her his name was Clarence Leonard, that he was from Halifax, and that she had just met up with the North Nova Scotia Highlanders.

Since arriving in Holland, Canadian soldiers had seen the effects of starvation and years of deprivation on the Dutch people. But little did any of them expect to find a Canadian woman in such condition. Mona was greeted by fellow Canadians who eagerly shared their rations with her, treating her to white bread with honey and plum jam, and hot tea. The latter stood out in her memory, because of the cup of hot, weak tea that had been given to her just prior to her deportation from Amsterdam to Anrath Penitentiary. During her incarceration in Germany, the only drinks she'd had were water and ersatz coffee. The other gift that she'd remember for the rest of her life was from a young soldier who had received a care package from home. In it were some Moirs chocolates that he wanted to savour. But when he saw a Canadian woman—and a Nova Scotian, no less—in their midst, he gave her three of the last precious Moirs chocolates, made in Bedford, Nova Scotia, to remind her of home. After years of deprivation, Mona did not gobble them up. She cradled them in the palm of her hand for a while, inhaling the rich, chocolatey-sweet scent. But when they began to melt, she put them in her pocket in order to eat them little by little. In an attempt to follow the precautions necessary in a war zone, the soldiers asked her to wait for the arrival of an officer. But when she declined the invitation, they did not persist. Their instincts must have convinced them she was telling the truth. After receiving more clean bandages for her feet, she set out again.

Her journey, though, was not to end so easily. When Mona flagged down a passing Polish transport, it took her to a clearing station. Although she repeated her story to some of the soldiers there, they were not as willing to accept her story without proof. Although no records from this time mention Mona specifically by name, it is worth noting that none of the reports for days around that time mention any civilians who were detained. But in the Canadian Army Ops Log, dated April 20, 1945, there are two significant lines provided by an infantry brigade with 21 Army Group in the vicinity where Mona was found: "Some enemy movement reported by listening posts. One civilian suspect being examined at Bde HQ."

After her ordeal, and the warm welcome she had received from members of the North Nova Scotia Highlanders just hours before, one can only imagine her confusion, and possibly even fear, upon encountering "friendly" soldiers who questioned her story. She could not prove she wasn't a spy, planted by the enemy in their midst. She had not even kept the papers provided by the Burgomeister of Rhede—which probably would have worked against her, since so many saboteurs had been provided with false identity papers by burgomeisters who retained belief that Nazi Germany could be victorious against the Allies. In light of these events and the intelligence reports mentioned previously, caution and the peculiar circumstances of war demanded that Mona be taken to Canadian Army Rear Headquarters for verification of her story. She was placed in the custody of an officer, and driven in a military vehicle to Oldenburg, Germany—not far from where she and Wendelien had started their trek near the end of March. In addition to answering questions for Canadian Military Intelligence, she was to receive more extensive medical care at a Canadian hospital unit there for the sores on her feet, which were badly infected.

In Oldenburg, another Canadian whom she had known in Wolfville learned of Mona's fate—Captain Robbins Elliott. He wrote at once to his parents in Wolfville on April 22 to share the astounding news. He knew that his father, in particular, would be interested to hear the story, because he had been the Parsons' family doctor when Mona was a young woman. Mona also met up with a few friends she knew from productions at Acadia in the 1920s—among them the doctor who treated her, Captain Kelly McLean, as well as Vincent White, who'd shared the stage with her at Acadia as late as 1928, and Ralph Shaw. There can be little doubt that her presence caused quite a stir among Canadian soldiers and that her story gave a boost to morale in the last days of the war.

Although delighted to be among familiar faces, Mona wanted very much to be back in Holland and to find out how her husband, their home, and their friends had fared during the war. But she had to wait at the Canadian hospital unit until Holland had been liberated and the military deemed it safe to return. The surrender was signed at a bombed-out hotel in Wageningen, Holland on May 5, 1945. Shortly after that, Mona was on her way home to Laren.

CAST OF CHARACTERS

Biff	Theodore Taylor
Buddy	Henry Whitney
Abie	Gordon Rose
Johnny	Lloyd Jenkins
Rube	Vincent White
Babe	Blair Fraser
Sonny	Bernard Cross
Pete	William McLean
Madame Benoit	Marguerite Milner
Marie	Margaret Porter
Babette	Virginia McLean
Julie	Mona Parsons
Alphonse Pettibois	Charles Coy
Louise Maitland	Marion Read

SYNOPSIS

Act I.—The courtyard of the Home of Madame Benoit
  Somewhere in Brittany.
Act II.—The same afternoon.
Act III.—That Evening.

MUSICAL SYNOPSIS

Overture - - - - The Orchestra
Act I.
  "Italie"—"My Buddies".
  "Please Learn to Love" - Miss Parsons
  "Darling I" - Mr. Cross and Mr. Fraser
  "Italie"—"My Buddies".
Entr'acte:— (a) "Please Learn to Love"
           (b) "Darling I"
Act II.
  "My Indispensable Girl" - Miss Read and Mr. Cross
  "Fairy Tales" - Miss Parsons and Miss Read
  Incidental—"Please Learn to Love"
Entr'acte:— (a) "Fairy Tales"
           (b) "My Indispensable Girl"
Act III.
  Twilight Song—"The Homes They Hold so Dear"
           - Mr. Fenton Elliot
  "Hullo Home"
  Incidental—"Please Learn to Love"
  "To be Together is the Main Thing" -
           - Miss Read and Mr. Cross
Exit March—Hullo Home.

Found without papers in newly-liberated Holland, Mona was taken to Canadian Army headquarters, where she met friends who recognized her from theatrical productions at Acadia in Wolfville—including soldier Vincent White, who shared the stage with Mona in the 1928 musical *Buddies*.

Above: the Dutch greet their Canadian liberators, 1944.

Right: Canadian 3rd Division ferries through a flooded area in Holland, 1944.

Wandering along the border area of newly-liberated Holland, Mona approached the first Allied soldier she saw: Clarence White of the North Nova Scotia Highlanders. Since the war, Canadians are still respected and loved by the Dutch for fighting to liberate the country and to bring food to a starving nation. *Above*: in Holland the Canadian task was to clear the channel ports. This was made more difficult by having to fight through large tracks of waterlogged and muddy lands, laid to waste by the Nazi invaders.

Chapter Thirteen

"*Welkum*"

Allan Kent was 30 years old and a crack journalist when he met Mona Parsons Leonhardt in April 1945. As war correspondent for Toronto's *Evening Telegram*, Kent knew that Mona's story would create tremendous interest for the paper's readers. But he had another reason for wanting an exclusive interview. He was a native of Halifax and had started his journalism career with *The Halifax Chronicle*. His tour of duty in Europe had started as a pilot with the Royal Canadian Air Force in 1942, but he'd resigned his commission when military authorities asked him to become a war correspondent. The story of a Nova Scotia woman's incredible spirit and tremendous will to survive had garnered a special place in the hearts of every Nova Scotian soldier who heard about her, and Kent was no exception.

He met Mona at her billet at a Polish women's camp, where she was awaiting transport to Holland. He was struck not only by Mona's courage and strength, but by the fire within her which could still be discerned despite her painful thinness, and by small details he attributed to years of deprivation and imprisonment. He recounted in his newspaper article her habit of moistening her fingertips to gather up tiny grains of sugar dropped on a table and of picking remnants of a chocolate-covered caramel from among the bits of lint in the pocket where she had tucked the precious morsel. When he pointed these out to her, she laughed. "I know I don't need to any more. I know upstairs I have a whole box of chocolates. But let me have my fun, won't you? Let me get my guilty thrill. A month ago these crumbs of caramel would have meant everything to me."

Because Mona had been such a boost to morale and had gained the admiration of so many Canadian soldiers, Kent had no problem commandeering a captured German military Mercedes to drive her home only a few days after their first meeting. During the journey she confessed to feeling ill about the prospect that her house might have been destroyed during the war. She was overjoyed to see the house still intact, and she made a beeline for the gardens, which she'd described to Kent during their drive. He was a few paces behind her, and he saw her stop in her tracks as she rounded the corner of the house. Her gardens had been torn up, and partly replaced with vegetables to feed the officers who had occupied the house. Mona surveyed the scene silently and soberly, then remarked to Kent that under the circumstances they would probably be glad of some vegetables in the months to come. She then turned on her heel and returned to the front of the house. A sign inscribed *Welkum* was draped over the front door by friends and neighbours, to herald her return.

The door opened and a big black dog romped down the path. Mona opened her arms, leaned forward and joyously cried "Brutus!" as the dog nearly knocked her over, covering her with sloppy kisses. She'd had two dogs at the beginning of the war, but only Brutus had survived, cared for by loving friends and neighbours. The dog was closely followed by Mona's housekeeper, Bep. Shortly after, a retinue of people including Georg Leonhardt, Jr., his wife Trüdl and their three children, friends, and neighbours gathered at Ingleside. Among the group were Lie van Oldenborgh and her husband. Everyone surrounded Mona, talking at once, hugging, laughing, crying, but the mood turned sombre for a minute or two when Mona eagerly inquired if Willem had come home. No word had yet been received about his fate.

The group moved into the house and the sight that greeted them deeply moved even Allan Kent, who had seen so much heartbreak in his tour as a war correspondent. Friends and neighbours had filled the house with spring flowers in anticipation of Mona's homecoming since learning she was alive. As blooms had wilted, they had been replaced with fresh, and the ritual continued until Mona stood once again in her own home, among familiar, friendly faces. Small amounts of liquor, which had been stashed away until there was a reason to celebrate, were produced for all to share, along with whatever food could be procured. Lie proudly returned the stash of articles she had buried for Mona nearly four years before.

Kent recounted, "These were well-to-do young Amsterdam couples—some of them, indeed, extremely wealthy—but to Mona Parsons they looked much thinner than when she had seen them last. They made light, however, of their own hunger and difficulties. Speaking in English that has slipped a little through disuse, they told her of the many plans laid for her escape—how they and others had contributed vast sums of money to men who promised to effect her release, and had just pocketed the money and done nothing, how once she would have found herself free except for the untimely vigilance of a Nazi guard, and how that attempt had cost the life of the man sent to accomplish it."

The days following her homecoming were anxious for Mona, as she hoped for news of Willem. Ironically, one of the first people to learn his whereabouts was Colonel Norval Parsons, in Sunny Brae, Pictou County, Nova Scotia. Willem had been liberated from a German concentration camp by Americans, and while receiving medical treatment, served as translator for the Americans. Willem was able to send a cable to his father-in-law in Nova Scotia via American channels, telling him he looked forward to returning home as soon as possible, and wondering if Norval had heard from Mona. Norval advised Willem that she was in Laren, awaiting his return.

Gustav Leonhardt recalls that a few weeks after Mona's return to Laren, Willem returned home in a quieter fashion. Gustav's family had gathered at his grandparents home in s'Graveland for a visit. Although the house was very large, the Leonhardts found little reason to lock their doors. Gustav recalls hearing someone call out, but that the voice was unintelligible, drawing closer to the room in which they were, and hallooing at intervals. Finally,

they recognized the voice of a family friend, a Mr. Heybroek. He
opened the door of the room and said quietly, "I have someone
here for you to see." He then stepped to one side and swung the
door fully open to reveal Willem Leonhardt standing behind
him. Later, Willem telephoned Mona to tell her he would soon
be with her.

Once united, the couple spent dizzying time together recount-
ing some of what they had been through over the last four years.
They were at last able to fill in some of the missing pieces for
one another—the length of time between Willem's capture and
Mona's trial (less than 12 hours), where Mona had been moved
when they had lost written contact with one another (the labour
camp at Wiedenbrück in 1944). Mona had begun to gain back
some of the weight she had lost, and was looking healthy compared to Willem, who was terribly thin and weak. His constitu-
tion could never have been described as robust, and the war had
reduced him to almost a shadow. Mona was attentive, minister-
ing to his needs until he regained some of his strength. They
spoke only as much as was necessary about what they had
endured. To do more, they feared, would raise the ghosts they so
keenly wished to lay to rest.

They found solace in plans to return Ingleside to its pre-war
condition. Many people who were connected with the resistance
movement had their homes destroyed by infuriated Nazis.
Family heirlooms and art works were plundered and stolen,
houses were burned to the ground. Remarkably, Mona and
Willem's home was virtually spared, mostly due to the vigilance
of their housekeeper, Bep. Almost everything that had been left
in the house, with the exception of a few silver, copper, and
pewter pieces, was returned to the Leonhardts at the end of the
war, along with the furniture removed by Georg Leonhardt, Jr.
One of Mona's most treasured possessions had remained in the
house, but did not come through the war entirely unscathed: her
piano. But, like the garden, she found she could be philosophical
about its condition. "At least," she consoled herself, "I lived to
see it again."

In the early months following the war's end, Mona received
two citations. The first, signed by Air Chief Marshall Lord

Tedder of the Royal Air Force, was on behalf of the British people, thanking her for her role in aiding members of the Allied
forces to evade capture. The second was signed by General
Dwight Eisenhower, expressing the gratitude of the American
people. While certainly proud and honoured to receive them, the
citations were yet another reminder of a chapter in Mona's life
which she wished to consign to the scrapbook. Life, she had
learned, was even more precious than she had imagined. It were
as though she had been given a second chance at it, and she was
intent on embracing it fully.

The President
OF THE UNITED STATES OF AMERICA
has directed me to express to
MONA LEONHARDT
*the gratitude and appreciation of the
American people for gallant service
in assisting the escape of Allied
soldiers from the enemy*

DWIGHT D. EISENHOWER
General of the Army
Commanding General United States Forces European Theater

This certificate is awarded to

Mrs. Leonhardt

*as a token of gratitude for and appreciation
of the help given to the Sailors, Soldiers
and Airmen of the British Commonwealth
of Nations, which enabled them to escape
from, or evade capture by the enemy.*

*Air Chief Marshal,
Deputy Supreme Commander,
Allied Expeditionary Force*

1939-1945

After the war, Mona Parsons received citations for her resistance efforts from both the British and American governments.

Chapter Fourteen

"grubbing weeds from gravel paths"

The work of cleaning and restoring the house and gardens at Ingleside to their pre-war glory took plenty of time and effort, and occupied Mona and Willem for the first months after war's end. In some places, the Leonhardts not only cleaned, but renovated and redecorated. One room to receive particular attention was the bathroom on the second floor. Wendelien, while dining with the Leonhardts the year after the war's end, had occasion to use the bathroom and was, as she recounted to her father in a letter written shortly after her visit, "astounded" by the colour scheme—pink and purple. So unusual was the decor that Wendelien decided that the fixtures and fittings could have come only from the United States, since such a colour palette was hardly the norm in post-war Europe. Years later, Wendelien mused that such extravagance was an important indicator of two things: first, the Leonhardts' finances were on solid footing despite the war; and, the significant bathroom renovation Mona and Willem had undertaken might have been inspired by bathroom facilities that were, at best, primitive during nearly four years of incarceration.

Mona also lavished loving attention on her gardens. Many trees and shrubs had suffered severe neglect during her absence. The lush lawn behind the house had been torn up and replaced by a vegetable garden. Weeds had all but choked her precious roses, and many of the trees she'd planted in 1938 had been hacked down, presumably for firewood. Although the deep pink rhododendrons had bloomed each spring that Mona was gone, the bushes themselves had become spindly and thin. With help from her gardener, she set to work restoring the grounds to their pre-war condition, reseeding the lawns, replanting flowers, trees, and shrubs, and pruning those that could be rescued. Like her father, Mona was an avid horticulturist. Her joy and pride in her gardens were evident in the results with which they rewarded her. Today, more than fifty years after the war, one can stand in the gardens in Laren and feel her presence still, moving among the rhododendrons, along the pergola, by the pond. The hours spent there must also have been a therapy, helping to restore a psyche that, like the garden, had been abused, ravaged, and scarred by the war, but never entirely defeated.

With the war over, Mona was at last free to visit her family in Nova Scotia. Although Willem was in delicate health, he decided to accompany Mona. The Leonhardts sailed for Canada, perhaps as early as the fall of 1945. Shortly after returning to Laren at the end of the war, Willem had met with his brother and told him that he had no further desire to be involved with Peck & Company In spite of this, the Leonhardts were sufficiently well off to allow Willem to travel with Mona and remain out of the country for a significant period of time. They took time to visit the United States, where friends had been so helpful in passing on Mona's letters to her father during 1940-41, prior to her arrest. They also enjoyed a lengthy visit with Alma and Norval in Sunny Brae. Mona's presence in Sunny Brae a year after the war inspired anecdotes still enjoyed today. A child at the time, Jane Evans was watching her mother weed their garden in Sunny Brae, when Mona walked by. Mona stopped, and commenting on the efforts, she quoted a line from Rudyard Kipling's "The Glory of the Garden"—"Grubbing weeds from gravel paths with broken dinner knives"—as a means of introduction, and then chatted pleasantly before continuing on her way. Local children also delighted in the unaffected and simple way in which Mona, when greeting them, would use her hand as a puppet, with the mouth formed by using the thumb as the bottom lip against a bent forefinger, which served as the upper lip.

There was hardly a resident in Sunny Brae who didn't know about Mona, her marriage, her station in Dutch society, and her treatment during the war. Those who expected to find a refined and haughty woman in their midst were pleasantly surprised— and probably relieved. Mona was as down-to-earth as anyone in the region.

In those days, there was only one cab driver in Sunny Brae. A man who enjoyed a tipple, the cabby frequently had his license suspended and local residents quietly marvelled that he could get it back so soon after his offence, usually after a quick trip to Halifax with Norval Parsons, who was known to have friends in the justice department. Requiring a taxi one night after visiting friends, Mona found herself in the vehicle of the notorious man. After climbing into the back seat, she announced that she could smell alcohol. Embarrassed, the driver confessed that he had open liquor in the car. Mona asked for a drink. Taken aback, the cabby said he didn't have a glass for Mona to drink from. Without missing a beat, Mona extended her hand over the back of the seat and said, "That's okay. Who needs a glass?" Delighted, the cabby passed back the bottle and Mona sipped from it as though from the finest crystal.

By May 1946, Mona and Willem were back in Holland. In mid-May, Willem gave a statement to RIOD to help incriminate three Dutch citizens who had worked for the Nazis by rounding up resistance workers. Mona visited Sunny Brae again in November 1948, with her brother Ross, for a surprise party to honour Norval Parsons. Members of Norval's former regiment gathered in Sunny Brae for a reunion with their former commanding officer. It marked the last time Mona would see her father before his death two years later.

Mona and Willem's attempts to restore their pre-war life was marred by Willem's precarious health, which prevented him from embracing life with the same gusto he once had. Trips to Bircher-Benner's clinic in Zürich continued to play an important part in their lives, and they continued to enjoy vacations on the continent each year. Willem's health did not prevent him from working. In his statement to RIOD in May 1946, he lists himself as having "no occupation," but several sources (including

Wendelien) report that he became an executive with the Bols Royal Distillers in Amsterdam. Whatever Willem's occupation, his source of income allowed the Leonhardts to enjoy the superior standard of living to which they had been accustomed before the war.

Mona continued to focus on her home and gardens, but also began giving more time to activities beyond Ingleside. Possibly inspired by her wartime experiences and her increased facility with the Dutch language, Mona became active in an amateur theatrical group in Laren, along with two very good friends, Max and Noor Zeylstra. The Leonhardts also resumed some of their favourite pursuits, such as dining and dancing in Amsterdam, though on a less frequent basis. They hosted some lavish evenings of entertainment at Ingleside, including appearances by the Leonhardt Consort, a classical music group headed by Willem's nephew Gustav. Among the guests at these soirées were Canadians serving as diplomats or senior military officers in Europe, and their spouses. Even after the experiences in Nazi prisons, Mona was a gracious, attentive, and animated hostess, full of humour and vitality.

No matter how much the Leonhardts tried to put their wartime experiences behind them, however, they would not be denied. Willem's health declined rapidly, becoming a grave concern by the early 1950s. Mona's predisposition to respiratory infections was made worse by conditions during her imprisonment in Germany. She suffered bouts of illness from which she had difficulty recovering. In a letter to Alma in March 1954, Mona says that not only had they been without a servant for four months, but also that both she and Willem were ill. Evidently Willem was in need of more attention, because Mona was receiving two injections of penicillin each week, in an effort to get rid of the infection to enable her to look after Willem, the dogs, and the household.

Although Mona slowly recovered, Willem's condition deteriorated and he was admitted to hospital on May 10, 1954. Ten days later, he underwent surgery to remove a tumour the size of a grapefruit from an area close to an artery in the upper leg—a procedure which required making an incision about thirty centimetres long. His kidneys were working in a diminished capacity, so the doctors could not administer a general anaesthetic. Afterwards, his leg was placed in a cast and elevated for a month. His leg was massaged frequently in an effort to help restore and maintain circulation, but Willem was in great discomfort, and Mona travelled to Amsterdam each day to be at his bedside. He began to show signs of improvement, though elevated levels of urea in his blood continued to concern both his doctors and Mona.

In October 1954, Mona's brother Ross, and his wife Mary, visited Mona and Willem for a few weeks en route to Johannesburg, South Africa. Willem had recovered sufficiently to accompany Mona, Ross, and Mary on various short trips around Holland. They went on canal boat tours, and visited the Rijksmuseum in Amsterdam, where they marvelled at Rembrandt's "Night Watch." Mona took them to the Staatmuseum, which at that time was housed in a mansion that had once belonged to a wealthy Portuguese banker, and which had been used by the Dutch Royal family for various state occasions. Mona told a museum official that her brother and his wife were visitors from Canada and, with the same desire to demonstrate warmth to Canadians that is shown today, they were ushered to a room not usually open to the public. It contained chairs once used during a visit by the King and Queen of Denmark. Mary reported that Ross sat in the chair used by Prince Bernhard, she in the one occupied by Queen Juliana, and Mona in the one used by the Queen of Denmark.

Because Ross and Mary had no plans to stop elsewhere on the continent, Mona convinced them that they had to take time to visit Paris. So adamant was she that she offered to take the train with them and show them the highlights of the city. Willem begged to remain at home in Laren, not feeling up to the long trip, and the trio happily set out for a fun-filled few days. That they enjoyed themselves is evident in a postcard sent to Alma, on which each of them managed to cram a few words about the great time they were having. On the train back to Amsterdam, they found themselves seated with a young married couple. As often happened in the years following the war, talk turned to

Family visits after the war. *Top*: Mona (with dog), Ross Parsons, his wife Mary, and William Leonhardt, during her brother's visit to Ingleside in October 1955. *Centre*: Mona and her brother Ross. *Bottom*: Norval and second wife Alma Parsons, on Mona's visit to Nova Scotia shortly after the war.

where one had been for the duration. Ross, who was conversing with the man, said that Mona had been in a Nazi prison and had escaped with a young Dutch baroness. Excitedly, the young man asked the name of the baroness. Mona was stunned when the man exclaimed, "Her fiancé was my wife's brother!"

During another trip, this time from Die Schwarzwald in Germany, Mona struck up a conversation with seatmates, only to discover that one of the men was a cousin of the prison director at Vechta. He remembered hearing his cousin talk about Mona and Wendelien, and wonder whether they had survived, because an order was issued by SS guards at the prison that they should be shot rather than recaptured. He was delighted that he would be able to tell her that both Mona and Wendelien had made it home to Holland.

Despite the messages in postcards to Alma during Ross and Mary's visit to Mona and Willem, all was not well. Mona had been sick before they arrived, and shortly after they left for Johannesburg, she was struck down again with respiratory illness. Writing from Johannesburg, Mary told Alma that Mona was looking tired and was not sleeping well. She also said that Willem, despite efforts to take part in their visit, was not able to join them downstairs much before 11:00 each morning, and that he had to spend most of his time in a quiet activity, like reading. She adds that "he really isn't at all well and eats practically nothing. Evidently he has a tummy upset every morning—yet he will drink. I don't know—perhaps he has to in order to keep going!" By the time Mary wrote this letter on November 24, she had discovered that Mona had been bed-ridden since three days after they had left Laren for Johannesburg. Suffering from a high fever and bronchial pneumonia, Mona lost more than eight pounds and was again having daily penicillin injections. The treatment continued for ten days, after which her doctor ordered a further ten days of bed rest, then three weeks at the Bircher-Benner clinic in Zürich to complete the recovery. Willem, whose health problems were compounded by dysentery at this time, was to accompany her.

Their years in German prisons had left both Mona and Willem in poor health, and they made several visits after the war to Dr. Max Bircher-Benner's renowned (and pricey) clinic in Zürich, Switzerland.

Chapter Fifteen

"a cracked crock"

By April 1956, Willem's health was extremely poor. Abuse he had suffered in prisons and concentration camps during the war had made him more susceptible to illness. He died in an Amsterdam hospital on April 8, 1956. Although Mona knew he couldn't live very long, she was devastated by his death. And she was entirely unprepared for the series of events which followed it. The full extent of these occurrences is not known, but even the sketchy details that have survived provide sufficient details to give insight into Mona's disbelief and mounting frustration as she tried to navigate Dutch bureaucracy.

Though there is confusion about what happened in the wake of Willem's death, one thing is certain: at the time, Dutch law prevented non-Dutch citizens from inheriting property. And though Mona had lived in Holland for 19 years—indeed, though she had gone to prison for nearly four years for her efforts during the war—she still wasn't a Dutch citizen. Mona's stepson, Tony Foster, claimed that after Willem's death, a woman came forth who claimed that she had given birth to an illegitimate son by Willem in the late 1920s or early 1930s. Victoria Tufts says she met the young man in question after the war at the Leonhardts' residence, though there is nothing to substantiate this story—a story further complicated by Foster's claim that the illegitimate child was concocted by the Leonhardt family to ensure that Mona would receive nothing from Willem's estate. But Mona's other stepson, David Foster, presents a much simpler, but no less unfortunate story, which he learned from Mona during her marriage to Harry Foster. "Mona by then had lost any urgent sense of time," he says. "She had been fighting since Billy Leonhardt died for her widow's share of the estate, and the Dutch government of the time, newly deprived of the wealth the East Indies had represented, through every means blocked her way so as to keep the money in the Netherlands. She simply had to wear them down. Unfortunately they wore her down." Certainly a less dramatic, but highly plausible and simple explanation of events.

A few of the letters Mona sent to Alma between May and October 1957 indicate that Mona was under a great deal of pressure, and that her health had suffered considerably. She was forced to move out of Ingleside on May 5, 1957, in part to pay substantial death taxes following Willem's death, and took up residence at the Hotel Jan Tabak in Bussum, not far from Laren. After living in the large, well-appointed residence she and Willem had called home for almost 20 years, Mona Parsons Leonhardt was living in "a room and tiny bath." It was, at least, a step up from the Nazi prisons cells she had lived in during her more than four years of incarceration. In the same letter to Alma, dated May 27, 1957, she writes that she is "All run down." In fact, she had been bedridden for two weeks with "grippe, bronchitis, laryngitis, and sinus infection" and her blood pressure was low. Although her doctor advised her to continue bed rest for an additional two weeks and then go to the Bircher-Benner clinic for two months, Mona's changed situation did not provide her with enough money to follow this advice. It's little wonder that she ended up in the condition she did—she wrote that she had worked literally day and night for three days in order to vacate Ingleside by the appointed time. In the final days she was reduced to sleeping on a bare mattress on the floor, without pillow or sheets, and with only coats for blankets. She vacated the house, but had to ask the new owners if she could store things in the garden house until she could move them or find buyers for them. Forced from her house, living in a foreign country which she had called home for most of her adult life (and for which she had served time in Nazi prisons), apparently ignored by her late husband's family, prevented from sharing in her husband's estate, Mona Parsons was deprived even of the companionship of her two dogs. Mona had friends who readily adopted one of the dogs, Caddy, but the other, Charmi, had to be taken to a kennel.

Mona's activities that summer are not known, though most of her time was likely spent in legal wrangling and investigations. By the end of September, her doctor had succeeded in persuading her to go to the clinic in Zürich, but once there Mona took umbrage at her treatment by nursing staff. Mona was at an extremely low ebb. Overwhelmed by legal and bureaucratic wrangling, and feeling extremely vulnerable by the time she arrived at the Zürich clinic, she bridled at what she deemed surliness on the part of staff who, she felt, ordered her about rather than gave her the gentle care she wanted. After a few days, she checked herself out, deciding that the best place for her was in the sunshine and fresh air of the Côte d'Azur and not in the starched, sterile environment of a clinic. The decision might have been a minor one, but definitely showed a spark of the pre-war, pre-widowed Mona.

Mona managed to meet up with friends, and wrote to Alma from Cannes that she had travelled there with a Dutch man and his Canadian wife, Mr. and Mrs. Jurjans. "Both they (the Jurjans), my doctor and lawyer...saw that I was ready for a collapse and 'crack up,'" Mona wrote to Alma, "so it seemed imperative that I get away from all worries and tasks for a while before more difficulties arise on my return, which must be faced." Her fighting spirit was renewed in Cannes. "You could never believe all the things that have happened to me. Very gruesome!" she wrote to Alma. "Even now they can't leave me in peace—even 'phoning from Holland to pester me with a lot of 'tricks' they're trying to put over while my lawyer is away. Had to write explanation (I sent a wire of 46 words) until 3:30 A.M. yesterday."

While Mona regained some of her strength, she decided she would not dissipate it by continuing her battle in Holland. She travelled from Cannes to the home of other friends in Tourettes-sur-Loup on October 15, then returned to the clinic in Zürich for a few days before returning to Holland. By the time she wrote Alma on October 25, Mona had not only made up her mind to return to Canada, but she had booked her passage to sail on December 8, 1957.

Exhausted and disheartened, Mona left Holland not only with her dignity intact, but also with personal possessions such as clothing, jewellery, linen, silver, and gifts from Willem and his family, including some furniture and her piano. She was not nearly as wealthy as she had been when Willem was alive, but she was still a woman of comfortable means, although she realized she would have to budget carefully. On her return to Canada, she took rooms at the Lord Nelson Hotel in Halifax until she found permanent accommodations: a modest apartment on Inglis Street. While living on Inglis Street she became reacquainted with Harry Foster, who happened to be a neighbour. They enjoyed spending time talking of their youth in the Valley, and reminiscing about dances at Camp Aldershot. They even talked of meeting one another in Holland while Harry was Commissioner of Canadian War Graves in the 1950s. But of all the images of Mona that Harry had carried through the years, the memory of a thin, ill Mona in a Canadian military hospital in Europe at the end of the war was one he could not shake.

According to Tony Foster in his book, *A Meeting of Generals*, Harry was feeling a bit like the forgotten man by the time Mona returned to Canada in 1957. He had retired from the military, and was learning firsthand that there's nobody like a former somebody. His military career over, widowed, living alone, and with his only two sons living in Ontario, Harry was at loose ends. According to his son Tony, Harry had found solace at the bottom of a bottle. And then Mona re-entered his life. Both were lonely and had been through their own personal wars, as well as the actual one. Life began to take on a little colour, a little light, even a little meaning. Mona was a natural performer and performers can't shine unless they have an audience—and Harry was a rapt audience. Mona joked to friends that there was more than a little truth in the old adage "Two can live as cheaply as one," when they decided to share their lives and one abode. Their reasons were not strictly economic, as both revelled in the fact that the other made them feel alive and eager to embrace life again.

In the garden behind the home of Harry's cousin Bill

Wickwire and his wife, Tig, Mona married Harry in June 1959. It was a happy occasion, attended by a handful of relatives and close friends. Bill and Tig's daughter, Gillian Wickwire Pullen, recounts that, although Mona's face was deeply lined and there was a sense about her of having "been through the wars," she was still vivacious and outgoing—as though her wartime experiences had fed the fire of her personality, rather than defeating her spirit. Gillian's observation was that "Mona had been born to fulfil that role in World War Two. She had a flair for drama; it gave her an identity, and she capitalized on it in order to survive. She hadn't got her break on Broadway, but she got it in the theatre of World War Two—that was her stage." Mona still played the part of the glamorous older friend, giving Gillian—as she had young women like Victoria Tufts and Shirley Elliot decades earlier—advice on clothing and comportment. "The way you sit is important," Gillian recalls Mona saying. She still remembers the way Mona would place herself in a chair. "Sit" just didn't do it justice. Her placement was perfect and graceful—long legs to one side, feet gracefully crossed at the ankles, forearms resting on the arms of the chair. Gillian was fascinated by this lovely, long-limbed, long-necked woman who, despite her years, had "great big eyes that would flitter and flutter" with great animation when she spoke. Mona's deep, sultry voice captured the young woman's attention, as did the ugliness of Mona's hands.

Like her arms, body, legs, and neck, Mona's hands were long. But any trace of grace they once carried had been compromised by the labour they were forced to perform during the war. The long hands seemed almost ungainly large, especially when the fingers ended in gnarls near the tips. The nails were thick and unhealthy as a result, Mona said, of having to spend work details digging cabbages out of the hard ground with her bare hands. Mona was almost embarrassed by her hands, but not so much that she refrained from gesturing when she spoke. And despite those poor, damaged hands, her gestures remained as graceful as the woman making them. The actor in Mona was able to use her unsightly hands to grace her speech, while at the same time ensuring that other, more pleasing attributes—her eyes, her voice—were the focus of attention.

Halifax as it would have appeared to Mona upon her return in the 1950s. *Clockwise from top*: Halifax Harbour, with the Citadel in the foreground; Mona arriving home from holidays, at "The Knoll," the Halifax house she shared with second husband Harry Foster; sailboats along the Northwest Arm.

The newlyweds moved to Rockwood Drive near the North West Arm in Halifax, where Mona gave the decor her distinctive flair. Gillian recalled that Mona had a way of arranging things— often items that wouldn't initially strike someone as "belonging together"—that gave the place a certain élan. Mona loved colour, though she didn't permit it to overwhelm her environment. She used it discreetly, in cushions, in rugs and other accents. And she still favoured clean, simple, and elegant lines in the overall design, while using flourishes and touches for dramatic focus and effect. Atop the piano, for example, Mona placed her large jewel case. While it was lovely, she didn't put it there to be admired while concealing its contents from view. Instead, she made it part of the decor by opening it and arranging it "with its contents cascading out" so that visitors could appreciate her discerning taste reflected in the baubles she had acquired—striking pieces of European design and, in some cases, of considerable karat weight.

Mona's clothes, too, were elegant. The outfits were designer, "beautifully tailored and crafted," says Gillian, and of exquisite quality, but older than those fashionable at the time, and perfectly suited to Mona's character and to her flair for the dramatic. Whereas some older women in similar clothes may appear eccentric or down-at-the-heel, no such label could be applied to Mona. She was unique and unabashed in her wardrobe, just as she was in her character, distinguishing herself anew as a gifted storyteller. She regaled Gillian with tales of meeting Willem and being swept off her feet to a wedding in Holland, and the high life they lived on the European continent in the late 1930s. Any bitterness Mona felt about bureaucratic entanglements following Willem's death did not diminish happy memories of her life with him. In fact, she was even a touch wistful when speaking of him.

Though Mona's circumstances were somewhat straitened, she was as generous as she had ever been. When Gillian and Hugh announced their engagement in 1967, Mona invited the bride-to-be over for a visit. Gillian arrived at the flat to find that Mona had strewn numerous items—silver, crystal, fine linens—on the sofa. She told Gillian to pick whatever she wanted. To this day, the silver oyster forks and the embroidered linen tablecloth and

napkins bearing the Leonhardts' initials are among her most treasured possessions.

From Rockwood, Mona and Harry moved to a small house at
Lobster Point, near the Chester Golf Club. Mona was delighted to
have a garden and a house with windows overlooking the
Atlantic Ocean. The Fosters entertained friends, enjoyed occasional visits from Harry's two sons, and travelled to Florida during the deepest, coldest months of the winter. Mona kept in
touch with old friends in Holland, mostly through Christmas
cards, and with Alma, who now lived only a few hours drive
away.

Although content in her new life, Mona's stepson David
believes that a part of Mona's spirit would forever remain in the
past. The couturier dresses from the 1920s, 30s, and 40s were
lovingly stored in a trunk. Sometimes, when the Fosters were to
entertain friends, Mona would retire to her room to prepare,
spending hours grooming and dressing, and inevitably would
have to be brought out of her reverie and reminiscences by a
knock at the door of her room to tell her that their guests had
arrived. David recalls once seeing Mona, who was bustling
about, stop at the trunk. She opened it and her entire demeanour
was transformed. Her purposeful movements dissolved as her
fingers touched one of the garments. She sat on the floor next to
the trunk and began to recount one of the times she wore the
dress, savouring each nuance of the memory as though it were a
wine of particularly excellent and rare vintage.

Both David and Tony recall times when Mona seemed overwhelmed by daily domestic tasks, frequently forgetting to do
things. Age wasn't a factor; she was only approaching sixty.
Instead, her priorities had shifted. Her years in prison, spent
focusing on basic survival, had given way to concentrated care of
a chronically-ill husband. And now, with no heavy demands on
her time, Mona allowed herself to drift on occasion. Grocery
shopping was one duty for which she seemed to have little affinity. She was never one to eat very much herself, and since she
had endured the deprivations and rationing of World War Two, it
was not unusual to find food spoiling in the refrigerator because
Mona could not bring herself to throw it out. David watched in

disbelief as Mona ate a rasher of bacon from the package—bacon which he had decided not an hour earlier was inedible because he had seen mould growing on it. But Mona simply scraped off the mould and ate the raw bacon, and then, noticing David's distaste, offered to cook the remaining slices for him.

While baking had once been one of Mona's favourite activities, and imagining recipes had helped her survive Nazi imprisonment, she seemed to have increasing difficulty coordinating the preparation of a meal. Tony describes taking his fiancée to Harry and Mona's for dinner. Mona had decided on a meal involving several courses, but plans quickly came unravelled. The meal was already cooking when Tony and Helen arrived at the house, and the four sat down to have cocktails. Mona had her usual sherry, and while they chatted, she slipped into the kitchen occasionally to check on the progress of the meal or to do the next step in the preparation process. But Mona loved to talk more than she loved to cook, and within a very short time, she had several cigarettes lit and burning in ashtrays in the living room and the kitchen, and was losing track of time. Harry kept the drinks coming, while Mona supplied more hors d'oeuvres, and the conversation sailed on. Eventually, they sat down to dine a few hours later. Mona, as usual, ate almost nothing, but made the table sparkle with her wit and her conversation.

Although Mona entered her early 60s during her marriage to Harry Foster, Tony recalls that her energy could leave younger people panting in her wake. He was astounded and delighted, during one visit to the Fosters' home in Chester, to see Mona entertaining a couple of her young neighbours by doing cartwheels on the front lawn. Although Mona was a heavy smoker, the toll cigarettes were taking on her lungs was not yet evident. For Harry, though, it was a different story.

In early spring 1964, Harry was plagued by a cold that would not get better, despite several attempts at bed rest, trips to the doctor and other cures. By the end of the spring, he was diagnosed with cancer and was admitted to Camp Hill Hospital in Halifax. In the wee hours of an August morning, Mona was roused from sleep in her bed at the home of Bill and Tig Wickwire (where she had been staying while Harry was in hospital) to be

Top: Mona and Harry Foster's house at Lobster Point, N.S., in 1962. *Bottom*: Mona and friends in Chester, N.S. "Taken 1965 by Alice Wickwire. You'll recognize me at the right, bracing myself to keep the chair on an even keel—therefore looking awkward, and with legs out of proportion. Brown Huntley is in the middle with her cocker 'Bonny,' and on the left is Alice's friend from Ottawa. This is the view from my front windows—we placed the chairs this way to have the nice background."

told that he had died. While relieved that his suffering was over, Mona was sorrowful to find herself on her own once more. Once again, widowhood would bring with it an additional blow, and again, it was one dealt by a government department—this time Canadian. She applied for a widow's portion of Harry's military pension and was turned down by Veterans' Affairs. Their reason for denying her application is unknown.

There is little information about her movements for the next year or so. She continued to live in the house she had occupied with Harry, and to occasionally travel back and forth to Halifax in her Austin Minor. In March 1966, she decided it was time to return to Holland to renew old friendships and see some familiar places. The prospect of the trip was exciting, and she eagerly anticipated it. In a letter to Alma, she joked, referring to an advertising campaign, that if Milly (Alma's sister) discovered "that Yardley's soap erases any wrinkles, to please let me know at once so I can erase mine before the Holland trip!"

She didn't confine her travels to Holland, but spent some time in England and in Belgium visiting Max and Noor Zeylstra. Also in Belgium were Wendelien van Boetzelaer (whose last name by then was—and still is—van Holthe) and her husband Han, and their children. The weather was warm, sunny, and pleasant for almost the entire duration of Mona's trip, and she returned home extremely happy and relaxed, pleased that the unpleasant memories of the past seemed to have been laid to rest at last, and that the trip had been devoted to celebrating happier times.

She arrived back in Canada in time to enjoy the rest of the summer, working in her garden and harvesting its vegetables. She wrote to her Dutch friends at Christmas, still warm with the memory of her visit with them, despite the icy blasts blowing off the north Atlantic that occasionally shook her house. In her note to Wendelien, she wrote that she'd had a minor car accident on icy roads while trying to make her way to Halifax one day—a mishap that left her without a vehicle for Christmas. She'd come to realize that living on her own outside the city would present some major drawbacks as she grew older. She wrote that her lease on the Chester property expired in May 1967 and that she'd decided to move back to Halifax, where she had not only old friends, but ready access to "good theatre, symphony and other concerts, lectures, art exhibitions, etc." as well as the universities if she decided to take "a course or two." At the end of her note, she adds "my breathing apparatus is none too good. They call it 'emphysema' and it bothers me a lot."

There is another long gap in communications and then, on New Year's Eve 1970, at five minutes before midnight, she began a late Christmas card to Wendelien, with whom she had lost touch since her visit in 1966. Mona got only as far as the end of the first paragraph, before she had to have a friend continue writing for her. Mona dictates, "I have been, and am still 'permanently ill' and it has to do with communication, especially with letter writing. This, my specialist forbids. I have had 26 'strokes' besides the big one with two blood clots, and what the doctor calls a very serious heart attack. Also emphysema. So you see, I'm really a 'cracked crock.' Two years ago I gave up alcohol (even sherry), coffee, and salt except for on eggs & potato. I gave up all social life, too, and now I'm an awful bore to myself. I even had to give up my dog as I could not look after him properly. My only recreation is very poor 'tele' as I cannot read properly since the strokes and attack."

Mona explained that she had decided to return to Wolfville, rather than move to Halifax because it had most of the same attractions Halifax offered, "but most of all, the old family cemetery plot is here, and it has, at the moment, four empty graves, and I intend to occupy one of them. It's nice to be handy & no one will need to tote me from anywhere." She concludes, "I doubt if I ever go again to Europe, but I do appreciate your kind invitation to stay with you. Thank you so much."

Although plagued by ill health, Mona still enjoyed the occasional walk along Wolfville's Main Street. Stopping to chat with those she knew, or even with those she didn't but whom she met in the shops, was something she enjoyed immensely. Marion Mapplebeck, who worked at the Royal Bank branch in Wolfville, recalled Mona's style. "She certainly stood out, but not in a gaudy or garish way. She had style and she wore clothes unlike I recall anyone else wearing in those days. She would visit the bank, and always looked stylish, dramatic, and terribly elegant."

Mona had rented the main floor of one of Wolfville's beautiful old homes—one that she likely saw many times as a young girl—at 444 Main Street. The house had a large garden and she enjoyed puttering around, planting flowers and ridding the beds of weeds. While working in the garden one day, she made the acquaintance of a young man who exchanged pleasantries with her as he passed by. He was Laun Ripley, a music student at Acadia. When she asked what instrument he played and he told her the piano, she was delighted, and invited him to play her grand piano. Mona had loved to play, but it had been one of the activities she was unable to do after her strokes. So it was a blessing when she found someone who would not only play for her, but played exquisitely. When not playing, Laun enjoyed tea with Mona, and listened to her stories with great interest.

Laun introduced Mona to his friend, Adrian Potter, who was a student at King's College in Halifax, but who was working in Wolfville for the summer. Much to Mona's delight, Adrian was a lover of great literature. Since reading was also denied her because of her strokes, Adrian readily agreed to visit her regularly to read from Dickens, Hardy, Dostoevsky, and the works of other great writers that graced her shelves. Their friendship, and the trust that came with it, grew rapidly. Soon Mona was comfortable with simply asking Adrian to let himself in through the unlocked door of her apartment. Several times, Adrian arrived to find that Mona was napping. By then, he was fully acquainted with her kitchen, and would make a pot of tea in anticipation of her waking. She learned which were his favourite tea treats, and made a point of buying some for him, even though the items were not permitted on her diet. Occasionally, when Adrian arrived, Mona would be awake, but in bed. She would call out to him from the bedroom, telling him she had bought some treats, but couldn't remember where she had put them. After some careful searching, Adrian was usually able to locate them, knowing that Mona would feel badly if he had been deprived.

Adrian also recalled the collection of couturier gowns Mona owned. In her Wolfville bedroom, she had wardrobe space that occupied one wall—room enough for her everyday clothing, and also for her gowns and furs. When the film *Man of La Mancha* premièred at the newly-renovated Acadia cinema on Main Street in 1972, Mona decided that they should make a real occasion of it, as she had done at many première and gala occasions in the past. She invited Adrian and Laun to get dressed up and attend the première with her. In anticipation, she shopped for special little delicacies and even purchased a bottle of champagne. The day of the première she prepared the canapés and put them in the refrigerator with the champagne. Then she began to prepare herself for the evening.

In the final years of her life, Mona never stepped out of the house without looking immaculately dressed and coifed. And the première of the *Man of La Mancha* was a particularly special occasion. Perhaps because of her rapidly-declining health, she knew that it might be one of the last times she would be able to put on the Ritz. When Adrian and Laun arrived at her apartment, they were stunned by the transformation. Mona had her hair done by one of the stylists in town and had applied her understated make up with particular care. She dressed in one of her couturier gowns, donned some of her most exquisite jewels, and draped a light mink wrap around her shoulders. "I know mink is hardly necessary in summer," she smiled with that sultry voice, "but I just want to let 'em know I've got it. So I decided on the wrap rather than the jacket." Mona had ordered a car so they wouldn't risk getting dust on their clothes on the walk downtown—besides, she didn't want to be tired by the time they reached the theatre. Although they found the film a disappointment, the three enjoyed themselves immensely. Afterwards, they returned to Mona's flat for canapés and champagne, and even Mona indulged in a little of the bubbly, though it was strictly forbidden by her doctor.

The occasion was one of the last where she was able to dazzle spectators with her elegance. Her emphysema incapacitated her more each month. Adrian returned to King's College in Halifax, but he visited Mona whenever possible during the school year and saw her more frequently in summer. He recalls that the oxygen tank and mask that were relegated to Mona's bedroom in the early days became her almost constant companion as time went on. Laun, though a gifted and spiritual musician, suffered from

In the late 1960s, Mona moved back to Wolfville—the hometown she'd left as a young woman—renting this ground-floor apartment at 444 Main Street.

schizophrenia and had agreed to be institutionalized at the suggestion of his family. While there, he hoarded his nightly sleeping pills until he had enough for a fatal overdose. Mona was devastated by his death—hardly surprising considering she had once fought so hard to preserve her own life when it seemed pointless to continue. The last time Adrian was able to see Mona before embarking on further studies to become a Russian orthodox priest, was during the summer of 1974—two years before her death.

There were few of Mona's friends left alive and in Wolfville by the mid-70s, although Mona's brother Ross and his wife Mary had retired to Bear River. When possible, she still ventured downtown, chatting with people she met. Most citizens of her generation, or slightly younger, knew what she had been through during World War Two, but there was another generation—those who would have been her grandchildren had she had any children of her own—who knew nothing about them. Whenever she lingered at a shop and told the young cashiers and clerks about having been imprisoned by the Nazis, and having escaped and walked barefoot across Germany to freedom, most were inclined to think of her as a senile old lady blessed with a terrific imagination. Although Mona had written an article about her experiences for magazine publication in 1960, she never wrote a book. Perhaps she thought that she would write her memoirs someday.

By the summer of 1976, Mona was almost completely bedridden and confined to her small apartment. The Eastern Kings Memorial Hospital was a short distance away, and on occasion Mona would call the switchboard when she was uncomfortable or having difficulty sleeping. Because it was a small town and the hospital staff knew her—and if the emergency ward was quiet—the doctor on duty would slip over to her house. Plagued by nightmares of her wartime experiences to the end of her life, weary of injections after so many years of receiving penicillin shots, and suspicious of sleeping pills, Mona was grateful simply for the doctor's company. One of the young doctors in the community played piano, so Mona was particularly grateful if he was on duty when she called the hospital. He had the compassion and the patience to sit with her and play softly some of her favourite, quiet pieces until she found a brief respite in sleep.

She received frequent visits from the Victorian Order of Nurses, so that she could remain in her own home as long as possible.

In the autumn of 1976 Mona developed a chest infection and, because it complicated her emphysema, she was admitted to the EKM Hospital. Her physical distress was occasionally relieved by brief periods of quiet. During bouts of delirium, she would awaken in her darkened room, believing herself back in a Nazi prison. Ross and Mary were among those who visited her, awaiting the inevitable. "Mona had a very rough life, a tough life," said Victoria Tufts Pickett, "but she had a spirit that could conquer anything. You would have liked her. I can't think of anyone who didn't like her. She was a survivor in every sense of the word." But on Sunday, November 28, 1976 Mona Louise Parsons Leonhardt Foster surrendered, probably for the first time in her life.

Described as "wife of Major General H.W. Foster," no mention is made of Mona's own wartime feats in the Wolfville cemetery where she is buried.

Ingleside, 1998: the garden Mona planted sixty years earlier continues to grow and bloom.

Epilogue

It is inappropriate to end a book—or anything else—about Mona Parsons with her death. While her physical body ceased its existence in November 1976, the most important parts of Mona—her spirit, her "life force" as Wendelien described it, and the memory of her—survive. Stand in front of Seminary House at Acadia University on a summer's day, and you'll sense her heading up the hill to her favourite, very private, sunbathing spot. Visit 444 Main Street on a rainy autumn night as the wind whips leaves off the trees, and you might glimpse her in the window, peering out at the storm just before she draws the curtains. Take your skates to the duck pond at Willow Park on a crisp winter afternoon and she'll be there, just out of the corner of your eye, gliding gracefully on the pond. Or maybe you'll find her strolling on the dykes, gazing out toward Cape Blomidon. Don't bother looking for her in Willowbank Cemetery—that's a place for the dead. And the memory of Mona Parsons—her vitality, her sense of humour, her drama—doesn't belong in a place like that. She visited many places in her life-time, and, with the possible exception of her garden in Laren, nowhere is she more tangible than in her hometown of Wolfville, Nova Scotia. But if you come seeking her, be patient. She reveals herself slowly and dramatically, ever the theatrical storyteller.